Consultant in History:
RODMAN WILSON PAUL
Professor of History,
California Institute of Technology

Consultant in Geography:
PHILLIP BACON
Professor of Geography,
Teachers College, Columbia University

ILLUSTRATED WITH PAINTINGS, PRINTS, DRAWINGS,
AND PHOTOGRAPHS OF THE PERIOD
MAPS BY VINCENT KOTSCHAR

THE GOLDEN BOOK OF
CALIFORNIA

FROM THE DAYS OF THE SPANISH EXPLORERS TO THE PRESENT

By Irwin Shapiro

GOLDEN PRESS · NEW YORK

Mrs. Reginald Walker

INTRODUCTION

Few states have had a history as colorful as California's. From the early Spanish explorers to the citizens of today, from *El Camino Real* to the freeways, from covered wagons to jet aircraft—something exciting has always been happening in this fascinating world on America's western shore.

This book tells the story of these happenings, and of the people who took part in them. Here are the padres of the missions, the dons and vaqueros of the ranchos, the miners of the Gold Rush, the mountain men, the Bear Flaggers, the vigilantes, and many more. Here, too, are tales of the destruction and rebuilding of San Francisco, of the Los Angeles land booms, of the construction of the trans-continental railroad, of the planting of vineyards and orange groves, of the rise of such industries as motion pictures, oil, and electronics.

The directness and simplicity of Mr. Shapiro's narrative will be welcomed by younger readers; it is dramatic and colorful enough to interest older readers as well. The illustrations, taken mainly from contemporary paintings, prints, drawings, and photographs, show how people and places actually looked at the time. This use of both words and pictures seems the ideal way to bring a region's past back to life. The many maps, especially made for this book, are still another aid to understanding California, both past and present.

In seeking pictures for illustrations, both Mr. Shapiro and I have been helped greatly by the directors and staffs of the Henry E. Huntington Library, the Southwest Museum, the Los Angeles County Museum, the California Historical Society, the Society of California Pioneers, the Bancroft Library, the historical department of the Title Insurance and Trust Company, and Mrs. Reginald Walker and Mr. Carl S. Dentzel, who kindly gave permission to reproduce material from their own collections. We are deeply grateful to them, and to the many government, civic, industrial, and business organizations who permitted us to use pictures in their possession. Picture sources are acknowledged in the credit line accompanying each picture.

RODMAN WILSON PAUL
Pasadena, California

Cover by Everett Henry
End sheets and title page by Douglas Gorsline

Los Angeles County Museum—Modern Enterprises

CONTENTS

Many early maps of America, like this one, showed California as an island.

The Sound of Bells

THE SPANISH COME TO CALIFORNIA

A few years after the discovery of America, a Spanish author wrote a story of strange adventures. In it he told about a far island—a wild, rocky island, shining with gold and precious stones. And he gave the island the name of California.

It was only a story, of course. At that time, there was no real California. But the Spanish could not forget the island, nor the beautiful name. California . . . the word had a golden sound, the sound of bells ringing in the sunlight.

And when Spain's soldiers and sailors explored the New World, that name stayed in their minds. Sailing up the west coast of America from Mexico, they came to a finger of land stretching into the sea. They thought it was an island, and they named it California.

Fortún Jimenez was the first white man to reach California, in 1533. On shore, he and twenty of his men were killed by Indians. The rest carried the news back to Hernando de Cortés, the military commander of Mexico. He was a mighty soldier who had conquered the Indians and brought Mexico under the rule of Spain.

Riches — gold, silver, precious stones — was what the Spanish were seeking. Hoping to find such treasure in California, Cortés himself went there in 1535. He found only a few pearls fished up from the bay. His men cursed him and the bare, dusty place, and after a little more than a year, they all returned to Mexico. But Cortés was still hopeful, and in 1539 he sent Francisco de Ulloa to explore the coast. Ulloa sailed up the Gulf of California and learned that this land was not an island, but a peninsula.

By 1542, the Spanish had sent to Mexico a new official—a viceroy, or governor. The viceroy gave Juan Rodríguez Cabrillo, a Portuguese, the command of two small, badly built ships. Cabrillo was to "examine the western side of California as far northward as possible." He was to look for "rich countries" and a way around North America to the Atlantic Ocean. Cabrillo set sail, and on September 28 he entered the harbor at San Diego. Rowing to shore, he saw a land where grass, trees, and flowers grew in "everlasting summer."

The Spanish called this land Alta California, or Upper California. They called the peninsula Baja California, or Lower California. It was Upper California that would later become part of the United States, and Cabrillo was its discoverer.

Cabrillo sailed northward, and at San Miguel Island he broke his arm. The bones did not heal, a sickness spread through him, and in January he died. But before his death, he asked Bartolomé Ferrelo to take command and sail on. Ferrelo reached the mouth of the Rogue River in Oregon, then made his way back to Mexico.

A different kind of visitor to California was Francis Drake, an Englishman. He was sailing the seas, raiding Spanish and Portuguese ships for their cargoes of gold and silver. His own ship, the *Golden Hind*, needed repairs, and in 1579 he anchored somewhere along the coast. The friendly Indians gave him presents of fish, feathers, acorns, and the skins of animals. Drake believed they thought him a god and wanted him to be their king.

He stayed for over a month, hunting and looking about, while his men cleaned and re-

On September 28, 1542, the explorer Cabrillo anchored his two ships in San Diego bay. He was the first European to land on Upper California.

paired the ship. During his visit, he nailed a brass plate to a post. The words cut into the brass claimed this land for Queen Elizabeth of England. Drake sailed west, completing a voyage around the world. He never came back to California, nor did the English ever try to settle there.

The Spanish made a few more voyages of exploration along the coast. They were especially anxious to find a good harbor. They had begun trade with the Philippine Islands, and once a year a large ship called a galleon journeyed to the Philippines. It brought silks, spices, and other goods of the East back to Mexico. The return trip was hard, and Spain needed a port in California where the galleon could stop for food, water, and protection from enemy raiders.

The most important voyage in search of a harbor was led by Sebastian Vizcaíno in 1602. He sailed for almost a year, until fearful rains and fog forced him to turn back. Some of his men died. His sailors were so weak from hunger and sickness that only two of them could climb the mast to the maintopsail. Somehow he managed to reach Mexico. He reported that there was a fine harbor for galleons at Monterey, and that it would be a good place for a settlement. But Mexico had a new viceroy, and this one saw no need for a port or a settlement in Upper California.

The land was left to the Indians, who lived as they had for centuries. A simple, easy-going people, they enjoyed games and singing more than war. They had never learned to farm. For food, they gathered acorns, roots, berries,

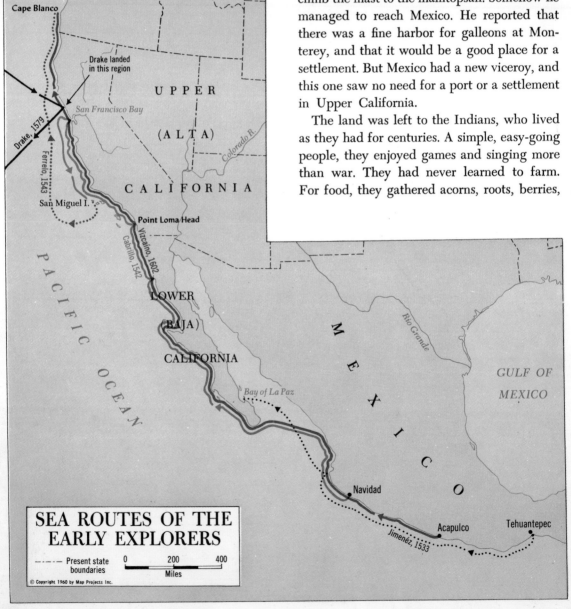

SEA ROUTES OF THE EARLY EXPLORERS

- - - - Present state boundaries

0   200   400
Miles

© Copyright 1960 by Map Projects Inc.

This brass plate was found in Marin County, north of San Francisco, in 1936. Many historians believe it was the plate nailed to a post by Francis Drake in 1579, claiming California for Queen Elizabeth of England. The holes at top and bottom could have been made by square nails. The large hole at lower right could have held a sixpence, an English coin with the head of Queen Elizabeth shown on one side.

Bancroft Library—Rendered by John Hull

When Drake stopped in California to clean and repair his ship, the Indians welcomed him and gave him presents of feathers and tobacco. In this picture, taken from an early French book, he is being crowned with a feathered headdress. Drake thought the Indians wanted him to be their king and rule over them. But it is more likely that they were simply going through their usual ceremonies to honor a stranger.

Southwest Museum

grass seeds, and insects. They also fished and hunted small animals. They had no pottery, but they were skillful at weaving baskets. They even cooked in baskets made water-tight with pitch or tar, dropping hot stones into the food to heat it.

For 167 years, except for a few voyages and pearl-fishing expeditions, the Spanish did nothing about Upper California. Meanwhile, Mexico City grew. On the vast Spanish lands in America, called New Spain, missions brought Christianity to the Indians. Settlers built pueblos, or towns. Soldiers guarded presidios, or forts. Father Eusebio Francisco Kino, a Jesuit priest, went exploring on horseback. With Father Juan María de Salvatierra, he

started many missions in Lower California.

Then the King of Spain learned that the Russians were crossing from eastern Siberia to the Pacific coast of North America. They planned to set up a colony in the land that would later be called Alaska. Who knew when they might decide to move south—south into California? The English and French, too, were dangerous. Their colonies in America had become strong and might spread westward.

José de Gálvez, the King's most important official in New Spain, believed that the Spanish must protect themselves by settling Upper California. He ordered that missions and presidios be built at San Diego and Monterey, and a third mission somewhere in between.

And so, in 1769, four parties of settlers left from Lower California. The first two parties went by sea, on the ships *San Carlos* and *San Antonio*. The vessels carried soldiers, sailors, cooks, blacksmiths, a baker, and all sorts of supplies. The other two parties went by land. They included soldiers and Indians who had become Christians. Traveling a wilderness without roads or trails, they drove pack mules, and herds of cattle and horses given them by the Lower California missions.

By July first, six months after the *San Carlos* set sail, all four parties were at San Diego. Sickness, accidents, hunger, and thirst had killed about a quarter of the men. Many of the Indians had run away. Less than half of

Father Junípero Serra

the three hundred men who had started reached San Diego.

One of the land parties was led by Captain Gaspar de Portolá, the commander of the entire expedition. In the same party was Father Junípero Serra, who was to be in charge of the missions in Upper California. Father Serra was not a young man, and he was not in the best of health. An old injury had left him with a lame leg. At the start of the trip, the leg was swollen and bothered him more than usual. But he refused to let that stop him and, on the way, a mule tender gave him some ointment used for mules. Father Serra rubbed it on his leg, and the swelling went down.

At San Diego, Father Serra prepared to hold church services and start a mission. From a framework of poles he hung a bell sent from Spain. And, in the land with the name like the golden sound of bells, a bell rang out in the sunlight. Many more mission bells would ring out in the land. Their sound was the signal that a new kind of life was beginning in Upper California.

A Chumash Indian village in 1542

In 1769 Portolá made camp where the city of Los Angeles stands today.

Along the King's Highway

THE FIRST MISSIONS AND SETTLEMENTS

Portolá had reached San Diego; now it was time to go on to the bay of Monterey. Again he divided his men into several parties. The few sailors still alive would sail the *San Antonio* back to Mexico, where they would pick up supplies and more men. Father Serra would remain here with the men who were too sick or weak to travel. Portolá himself would lead a party overland to Monterey.

At four o'clock of a hot afternoon in July, Portolá mounted his horse. Squinting in the sunlight, he stared at his little army. There were two priests, several officers, about thirty soldiers wearing leather jackets, fifteen Indians, and some muleteers and servants. Altogether, he had sixty-three men. They were so thin that they looked more like skeletons than living persons.

Well, whatever they looked like, they must do their duty. Portolá gave the command, and they set off. Driving a long line of a hundred pack mules, they moved northward along the coast. They felt an earthquake, crossed a river, crossed a mountain, came down into a valley.

They passed the bay of Monterey, but did not recognize it. They went on through a forest of giant redwoods, were soaked by cold rains, and came to a great harbor. They had discovered San Francisco Bay, which had somehow been missed by every explorer. It seemed large enough to shelter the navies of all Europe.

They knew that they had gone too far north, beyond Monterey. They had eaten most of their food, and Portolá decided to return to San Diego. For the last twelve days of their journey, they killed a mule each day and ate the meat. They reached San Diego on January 24, 1770, "smelling frightfully of mules," as Portolá later wrote.

More men had died at San Diego. The living were sick and hungry, for the *San Antonio* had not come back with supplies. Day after day, for nine months, the men watched for the ship. At last Portolá said that if it did not arrive by March 20 he would order the expedition back to Lower California.

The men kept watching for the ship. The priests prayed. Then, on the nineteenth of March, a shout went up: "A sail! A sail! It's the *San Antonio!*"

Quickly the smiling men unloaded the ship. There were medicines for the sick; corn, rice, and flour for the hungry. No longer would they have to trade their clothing to the Indians for geese or fish or other food.

In less than a month, the *San Antonio* sailed for Monterey. Portolá followed by land with sixteen soldiers. This time he found the bay without any trouble. On June 3, 1770, the flag of Spain was raised on the shore. A cross and an altar were set up, and two bells were hung from the branch of a huge oak tree. Again the bells rang out, and Father Serra held church services. And when the news was brought to Mexico, flags flew and bells rang there, too. A presidio and a mission would be built at Monterey—more than two hundred years after Cabrillo's discovery.

By 1773, Father Serra had started five missions. He traveled from one to another over *El Camino Real*—the King's Highway. Some day this would be a broad road running the length of California, but in 1773 it was just a narrow trail.

Walking along it, mile after mile, or riding a mule, Father Serra thought of the troubles of the new colony. For one thing, not enough Indians were coming to the missions. For another, there were not enough white settlers.

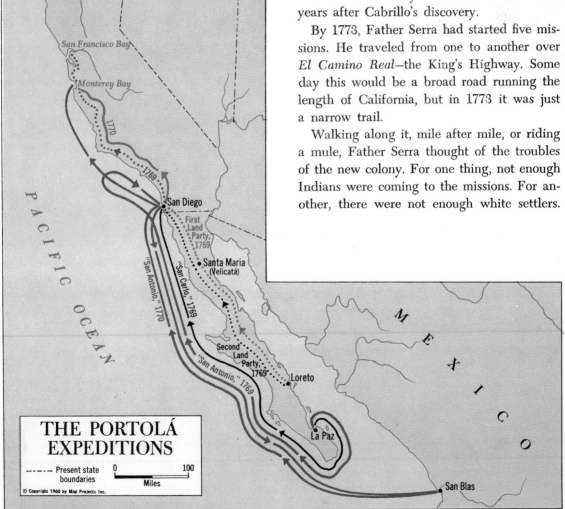

San Francisco Bay

Monterey Bay

1770

1769

PACIFIC OCEAN

San Diego

First Land Party, 1769

Santa Maria (Velicatá)

"San Antonio," 1770

"San Carlo," 1769

Second Land Party, 1769

"San Antonio," 1769

Loreto

La Paz

MEXICO

San Blas

THE PORTOLÁ EXPEDITIONS

- - - - Present state boundaries

0　　　100

Miles

© Copyright 1960 by Map Projects Inc.

Seeking a route from Mexico to California, Captain Anza found the desert rough going. But Father Garcés urged him on, and he reached San Gabriel.

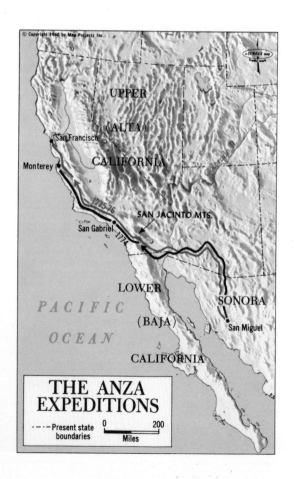

And then all supplies had to be brought in by ship from Mexico, and the voyage was long and dangerous. If California was to grow, a way had to be found to bring supplies and settlers from Mexico by land.

Luckily, Antonio María de Bucareli y Ursúa had become viceroy. Visiting him in Mexico, Father Serra learned that Bucareli was greatly interested in California. Bucareli, too, believed a land route must be found. More than that, he knew just the man to do it—Captain Juan Bautista de Anza. Before Father Serra returned to his missions, Bucareli ordered Captain Anza to lead an expedition to California.

Anza was an experienced soldier. He was the commander of a presidio at Tubac, in the part of Mexico called Sonora. He had long wanted to find a way to California, and he soon got together a band of twenty volunteers. With two priests and a few Indians, muleteers, and servants, they set out over the hot, dry desert. They came to a village of friendly Yuma Indians, who helped them cross the Gila and Colorado Rivers. They tramped over the sand dunes of another desert, but their horses and mules became so tired, hungry, and thirsty that they had to turn back. Then they tried again, and this time they got past the desert. Discovering a pass through the San Jacinto Mountains, they swung over and down the western side to the San Gabriel Mission. From here they marched up the King's Highway to Monterey.

Returning to Mexico, Anza gave Bucareli a report of his expedition. The Viceroy was delighted. Now settlers must be taken to California over the same route. Anza immediately began preparing for a second expedition, and at the end of September, 1775, he set out again from Sonora. He had a large party of 240 persons, including women and children, 695 horses and mules, and 355 head of cattle.

There were some hardships on the journey. In the desert beyond the Colorado River, the party ran into strange weather—cold and snow. Water was scarce. Many of the animals were lost. But only one person died on the 1500-mile trip. Three babies were born, one of them the first white child born in California. The party rested at the San Gabriel Mission, then went up the King's Highway to begin a settlement at San Francisco in 1776.

San Francisco was built around a mission and a presidio. A different kind of settlement— a pueblo, or town—was started the following year at San José. In 1781, a second pueblo was started by eleven families. They numbered forty-four persons, none of whom could read or write. Their settlement was called El Pueblo de Nuestra Señora la Reina de Los Angeles de Porciúncula — the City of Our Lady the Queen of the Angels of Porciúncula — which later was shortened to Los Angeles.

That same year something unexpected happened on the trail which Anza had opened up. The Yuma Indians, who had once been friendly, attacked two missions on the western side of the Colorado River. They burned the buildings, killed four priests and more than

The presidio, or fort, built at San Francisco to protect the settlers

thirty soldiers, and carried off the women and children going to California. For twenty years after that, no one dared to use the trail.

Even so, California went on growing. Father Serra still watched over the missions. Wearing sandals and a brown robe, limping, leaning on a staff, he walked from one to another, or rode a mule. For fifteen years he traveled the trail called the King's Highway. His health grew worse, and still he went on his journeys, confirming the Indians who had become Christians. Finally, in June of 1784, he felt he could travel no more. He made his way to the San Carlos Borromeo Mission at Monterey, which had become his home.

Father Serra was seventy years old, and tired. He knew he did not have much longer to live, but he was satisfied. As a boy he had wanted to work among the Indians of the New World, and he had had his wish. There were now nine missions along the King's Highway. More than six thousand Indians had been baptized; more than five thousand confirmed. There were about seven hundred white settlers, with four presidios to guard them.

In August of 1784, Father Serra died. Dressed in his brown robe, he was buried in the mission. Above him the mission bells rang slowly in mourning—the bells which he had helped to bring to California.

The Indians, usually friendly, sometimes attacked the settlers. In this old drawing, Spanish soldiers are fighting Indians with guns and lances.

Southwest Museum

Five bells called the Indians to prayer at the San Diego Mission.

Missions and Visitors

MEXICO TAKES OVER RULE OF CALIFORNIA

After Father Serra's death, other priests still traveled the King's Highway. They started four missions during the years of 1786 to 1791; five during 1797 and 1798. At first, the missions were merely huts of poles and mud. Then, as more Indians answered the call of the bells, fine new buildings were put up. They were made of adobe—a kind of mud—which was formed into bricks and dried in the sun. The walls were covered with plaster, the roofs with red tiles.

The missions had the use of many thousands of acres of land. They had gardens, orchards, vineyards, wheatfields, and pastures. They counted their horses by the hundreds, their cattle and sheep by the thousands. At one time, San José had 62,000 cattle, while San Luis Rey de Francia had 30,000 sheep.

The padres, as the priests were called, taught the Indians to pray, to understand a little Spanish—and to work. The Indians learned to plant and harvest crops, to build irrigation ditches, care for the animals, tan hides, and make cloth, pottery, and flour. They were given food, clothing, and shelter, but no pay.

When the bells rang in the morning or evening, they went to church. When the bells rang at noon, they ate. Those who would not work were punished. Those who ran away

Indians dancing in front of the San Francisco Mission. There were many different tribes of Indians in California, each with its own way of living.

were hunted through the hills by soldiers, brought back, and whipped. And always they were under the watchful eye of the padres.

Many of the Indians died of sickness. The year the Spanish first came to Upper California, there were probably about 130,000 Indians on the land. Between 1769 and the end of 1834, the padres baptized 89,800 Indians and buried 66,100. No more than 30,000 Indians ever lived at the missions at any one time, and usually less than that.

Meanwhile, life was becoming easier for the Spanish settlers. California had its own governor, appointed by the viceroy. The first two had not even wanted to live in Alta California, but, beginning in 1777, the governors lived at Monterey. Diego de Borcia, the seventh governor, wrote to a friend, "To live much and without care, come to Monterey. . . . This is a great country. . . . This is the most peaceful and quiet country in the world. . . ."

Meanwhile, too, visitors were coming to California from other lands. One was a Frenchman named La Pérouse, who was making a

voyage around the world for his government. He admired the mission fathers, but he thought they were not preparing the Indians to do things for themselves.

Captain George Vancouver, an Englishman, visited California three times. He thought that the Spanish could easily be pushed out of California by any nation that decided to attack them. And in 1796, Captain Ebenezer Dorr brought in the first American ship to enter California waters.

Ten years later, Nikolai Rezánof anchored his ship off San Francisco. He had come to get supplies for the Russian colony in Alaska. During his stay of six weeks, he met Concepción Argüello, the daughter of the commander of the presidio. Rezánof asked her to marry him. The wedding would take place as soon as he returned from a trip to Russia to see the Czar. He sailed away, and month after month, year after year, Concepción waited for her wedding day. At last she grew tired of waiting and became a nun. She never saw Rezánof again. Not until thirty-five years had passed did she learn that he had died in Siberia, while journeying to see the Czar.

In 1812, more Russians came down from Alaska—one hundred of them, with eighty Aleut Indians. They settled north of San Francisco, on a high rocky shelf overlooking the sea. They built Fort Rossiya, later called Fort Ross, protecting it with a high palisade of logs. A little town of sixty buildings, including a church, grew around the fort.

For a long time the Spanish had been afraid that the Russians would move into California. Now that it had finally happened, there was nothing they could do about it. Soldiers sent by the governor to scout the fort reported that the Russians had muskets, heavy cannon, and plenty of gunpowder. Luckily, the Russians did not try to make more settlements.

Art Riley

The wooden church (above) was used by the Russians at Fort Ross until 1841, when they gave up their colony and left California.

Roses and vines today cover the ruins of the San Juan Capistrano Mission (below), where the padres once planted beautiful gardens.

Union Pacific Railroad

They seemed satisfied with Fort Ross. They had come to America to catch sea otters and fur seals, and they were busy hunting and trapping and trading.

Ships from New England carried the furs across the Pacific, where they were sold to the Chinese. Soon many Yankee ships were putting in at the coast of California. Their captains began asking the Californians to sell them food for their crews and furs for the China Trade. Californians were forbidden by Spanish law from trading with foreigners, but there were ways to get around the law. They smuggled the skins of seals and sea otters out to the Yankee ships, in exchange for goods they could not get from Spain or Mexico.

The Californians were glad to trade with the Americans, and with the Russians at Fort Ross as well. Few supply ships were coming in from Mexico, where the Viceroy seemed to have forgotten about California. The truth was that he had troubles of his own. The Mexicans were tired of being ruled by Spain and there was bloodshed in the land.

MISSIONS
AND THE
CAMINO REAL

Dates indicate
establishment of Missions

0   100   200
Miles

San Francisco Solano, 1823
an Rafael, 1817
San Francisco, 1776
San Jose, 1797
Santa Clara, 1777
Santa Cruz, 1791
San Juan Bautista, 1797
San Carlos, 1770
Soledad, 1771
San Antonio, 1771
CAMINO REAL
San Miguel, 1797
San Luis Obispo, 1772
Purísima Concepción, 1787
Santa Inés, 1804
Santa Barbara, 1786
San Buenaventura, 1782
San Fernando, 1797
San Gabriel, 1771
San Juan Capistrano, 1776
San Luis Rey, 1798
San Diego, 1769
Yuma, 1780

© Copyright 1960 by Map Projects Inc.

California was too far away to get much news of Mexico's fight for independence, or to take sides in it. But on a November morning in 1818, cannon boomed from a ship in the bay of Monterey. They were fired by Hippolyte de Bouchard, a Frenchman commanding an Argentinian privateer in the wars against the King of Spain. The soldiers at the presidio fired back, then were forced to retreat. Bouchard's men went roaring into the town. After stealing everything they could, they set fire to the buildings. They made a few more stops along the coast, burning ranch buildings and the mission of San Juan Capistrano. They sailed away with their loot, and the little war was over.

In Mexico, the real war went on. Not until 1822 did the Californians learn that Mexico had thrown off the rule of Spain. This meant that California was no longer Spanish, but Mexican. At the presidios, Spain's red-and-gold flag was hauled down. It would be replaced by the new flag of Mexico—red, white, and green, with an eagle in the center.

The people of California were happy about the change. Now they could do away with the laws against trade, and perhaps get more protection against enemies. Three years later there was another change. Mexico became a republic, and California was one of its territories.

Mexico did not find it easy to rule the Californians. They were too independent, and they were too far away. Often they disliked their Mexican governors. Sometimes they fought the governors, and sometimes they fought among themselves. The fighting was mostly noise, marching, and loud speeches, with few men hurt or killed. At the Battle of Cahuenga Pass in 1845, the only casualties were one horse killed and one mule wounded.

More important than the fighting was a law passed by the Mexican government in 1833. Under this law, the land belonging to the missions was taken away and half of it divided among the Indians for farms. Just as La Pérouse had feared, the Indians had not been prepared to do things for themselves.

Los Angeles County Museum—Modern Enterprises

The first American flag in California (above), made from three shirts, was raised by New England sailors in 1829, over a shed in which they cleaned and stored hides before sailing.

They were used to obeying orders and did not know how to look after their own farms. They soon lost their lands to dishonest white men. They ran off to join the tribes that still remained in the wilderness, or they went to work for the white men.

Slowly, as the years passed, the padres left the missions, and there was no one to take care of the buildings. Worn away by the wind and the rain, the walls crumbled. With a clatter of tiles, the roofs fell in. Birds nested in the bell towers. And the bells themselves, that had once made a golden sound in the sunlight, were as silent as Father Serra's grave.

The Santa Barbara Mission (below) is known as the Queen of the Missions. In Spanish days, men, women, and children would greet their friends when they gathered at the church.

Southwest Museum

A Spanish ranchero and his major-domo, or household manager

The Californios

LIFE ON THE RANCHOS

Juan José Domínguez was an old "leather-jacket" soldier. He had come to California with the Portolá expedition, and he never forgot those days. He remembered Father Serra kneeling beside a dying Indian, and Portolá riding at the head of his men. He remembered the long march in search of Monterey, the taste of mule meat, the shouting when the supply ship anchored in the bay.

In 1784 he reached the age of sixty-five. He was too old for a soldier; it was time for him to retire. But he still had years to live, and he wanted to spend them raising cattle.

He would sit peacefully drinking wine under the warm sun, while his steers grazed on the little hills. But to do that, he needed land— land of his own.

Juan José and two other soldiers wrote to Governor Pedro Fages, who had been their captain, asking for grants of land. Fages agreed. And so the three old leather-jackets started the first ranchos, or ranches, in California, and became the first rancheros. Not many more grants were made while Spain ruled California. But after the Mexican Revolution and the breaking up of the missions,

Mrs. Reginald Walker

This painting by James Walker shows an early ranch house, built of adobe.

hundreds of new settlers were given tracts of from 4,500 to 50,000 acres of land.

The earliest rancheros built small and simple houses of adobe. They had little furniture, and the floors were just earth pounded flat. Later some of the rancheros tried to live like the dons, the noblemen of Spain. They built larger, more comfortable houses, big enough for a family that might have as many as fifteen or even twenty children. Nearby, there would be a number of smaller houses and huts. Several hundred people might live on one rancho —relatives of the owner, workers such as carpenters and tanners, Indian servants, and vaqueros. The vaqueros were the first cowboys in America. They were hard-riding horsemen, skillful with the reata—a lasso made of cowhide.

Ranchos had no fences, and the cattle roamed the valleys and rolling hills. Each

At rodeo time, the rancheros' long-horn cattle were counted and calves branded.

California Historical Society

Vaqueros, the first cowboys in America, rounding up a herd of horses

year, usually in spring, the rancheros invited their neighbors and friends to a rodeo, or roundup. Shouting, whooping, swinging their reatas, the vaqueros drove the cattle to the gathering place. Dust rose in a great cloud from the stamping hoofs of the herd. The vaqueros darted about on their swift ponies, separating the steers of their own ranch from the other cattle. Bellowing calves ran after their mothers. The vaqueros lassoed the calves and branded them with a hot iron.

Rodeos meant fun as well as work. When the cattle had been separated and the calves branded, there were horse races and games of skill and chance. A favorite game was *carrera del gallo,* the rooster pull. A live rooster was buried in the ground up to its head. Leaning from their saddles, horsemen tried to snatch up the rooster as they rode by.

In the evening, as the stars came out in the sky, fires were lit. The ranchero and his guests feasted on barbecued beef, tortillas, fruit, cake, and wine. They sang songs, told stories, and danced to the gay music of violins, flutes, and guitars.

After the rodeo, some of the cattle were turned loose to roam again on the open range. The rest were driven back to the ranchos, where they were killed. The hides were stretched out on the ground to dry in the

A Spanish horseman reaching for a rooster as he plays carrera del gallo, *one of the games that made the rodeo a happy, exciting time*

Indians did much of the work on a rancho. Here they are boiling down fat for tallow, which would be made into soap and candles.

sun. The fat was put into big pots and boiled down into tallow, which was used to make soap and candles.

Most of the work on a rancho was done by Indians. The rancheros spent many hours on horseback, riding about their lands. Often they went hunting with the vaqueros, to catch wild horses or grizzly bears. Lassoed by several men, the huge bears were sometimes dragged away and matched in fights against fierce bulls.

The door of the big house was always left open to travelers. Rancheros greeted friends or strangers with *"Mi Casa es suya"*—"My house is your house." And when they were

Riding across their lands, the rancheros often joined their vaqueros in catching wild horses or bears. The reatas, or lassos, were made of cowhide strips, which were first soaked in water, stretched, and dried. Then four strips were braided into a line strong enough to hold any animal.

The Californios, as the Spanish rancheros called themselves, were always ready for feasting and dancing. Weddings meant a big celebration, lasting for a week or even longer. The bride and groom were escorted home from the church with music (above). Dressed in silks, velvets, and broadcloth, the guests feasted at tables or beneath the trees. The food was often prepared by servants at outdoor ovens (below).

not entertaining travelers, they passed the time with *fiestas* and *fandangos*—celebrations and dances. Anything would do as an excuse for a fiesta. It might be a wedding, a church holiday, or just a gathering of friends. And so the sunny days passed to the rumble of hoofs, the jingle of spurs, the creak of saddle leather, and the nights to the sound of voices and the clang of guitars gleaming in the moonlight.

It was a good life, a slow, easy, peaceful life. The rancheros had no schools, no libraries, no newspapers; many of them could not even write their own names. They knew little of what was going on in the world. They did not think of themselves as Spanish, or American, or Mexican. California was their home, their land, their country, and they called themselves Californios.

The main link with the United States was the trading ships. Whenever a ranchero heard that a ship had arrived, he ordered his hides and bags of tallow loaded on a two-wheeled cart called a *carreta*. He rode to the shore, where he bargained with the ship captain for all sorts of goods—silk and shoes, furniture and fireworks, guns and knives and cigars. He paid for what he bought with hides and tallow. Seldom did any money change hands. In fact, very little money was seen at any time on a rancho. But the hides, which were worth from two to four dollars, were called "California bank notes" and "leather dollars."

Most of the trading ships came from New England. The first Yankee ships had come for smuggled furs. Then whaling vessels, homeward bound after a long voyage, began to stop at California for fresh food and water. In exchange they often left behind the big iron pots in which they boiled whale blubber. The pots were hauled to the ranchos and used for boiling down tallow. Soon Yankee captains began sailing ships to California just to do business with the rancheros.

The ships brought a new kind of settler to the land. As early as 1816, young Thomas Doak, a carpenter, came ashore from a smuggling ship at Monterey. He liked California so well that he decided to stay, becoming the first American settler. That same year, Daniel Call, who was also an American and a carpenter, settled in Santa Barbara.

Two years later, Joseph Chapman landed with Bouchard's pirates. Perhaps Chapman did not intend to stay. He and two others of the crew were lassoed with reatas, captured, and taken prisoner. "Blond Joe," as Chapman was called, remained in California. He said that he had been forced to join the pirates, and in time he was pardoned and freed.

Everyone liked him, and it seemed to the Californians that he could do anything. He could cut down trees, saw logs into boards, fix broken tools, and make soap. He could set broken bones, treat wounds, and pull teeth. He built grist mills for the missions at Santa Inés and San Gabriel, and constructed one of the first ships built in California. He took a band of Indians to the mountains near Pasadena, set up a lumber camp, and cut logs for the church that was being built in Los Angeles. He became a Catholic, married, and made his home in Los Angeles, where he planted a vineyard of four thousand vines. Later he moved to a large rancho in Santa Barbara.

As more ships came to trade, more Americans settled in California. Some worked as agents for the ships. Others became merchants or rancheros. Among them was Don Abel Stearns, who made himself the richest man in California.

Don Abel was not a handsome man, and people called him *Cara de Caballo*, or Horseface. Even so, he married Arcadia Bandini, who was widely known for her beauty. The vaqueros made up a song about them:

> *Two little doves sang in a laurel,*
> *How lovely Dona Arcadia,*
> *How ugly Don Abel!*

Like Don Abel, the Americans learned Spanish, joined the Catholic Church, and became citizens of Mexico. They lived and spoke and dressed like the other rancheros, and they, too, called themselves Californios.

A Yankee sea captain trading for hides with padres from the San Juan Capistrano Mission. Indians are unloading hides from a carreta, or oxcart.

Los Angeles County Museum—Modern Enterprises

The mountain men were trappers who roamed the West in the hunt for beaver.

Over the Mountains

BLAZING THE TRAIL TO CALIFORNIA

Far from the ranchos and missions, on the high slopes of the Rocky Mountains, roamed the mountain men. They were hunters and trappers who lived much like the Indians. Along the rivers and streams they set their traps for beaver, whose skins they sold to fur traders. As beaver became harder to find, they pushed farther and farther west. And in August of 1826, a party of mountain men set off toward the southwest on a journey that would take them to California.

They started from a meeting place northeast of Great Salt Lake, Utah. Before them lay strange, wild country, where no white man had ever traveled. They would have to find their own way, break their own trails.

But they were at home in the wilderness and they had no fear.

Besides, their leader, Jedediah Smith, was one of the wisest of the mountain men. A fur trader as well as a trapper, he and his two partners had prepared carefully for the journey. There were to be fifteen men in the party. On the backs of pack animals they carried knives, awls, beads, looking glasses, blankets, red ribbons, powder and lead, razors, rings, bells, combs, needles, and tobacco to give to the Indians. Smith was out to find new trapping grounds. Perhaps he also wanted to find a new path to the Pacific and to explore California and Oregon. Or perhaps, as he himself said later, he simply went southwest, found little beaver, and kept on going until he reached California.

Smith and his men worked their way past the eastern side of Great Salt Lake and Utah Lake, then through miles of dry, dusty country. At the Colorado River, they stopped in the villages of the Mojave Indians, staying fifteen days to rest and get fresh horses. Two Indians who had run away from the California missions went with them as guides.

Crossing the Colorado River, they came to a desert. Suddenly they seemed to be on another planet, where a tremendous sun poured heat from the blazing sky. There was not a tree to give them shade. The waterholes were far apart; the water itself was dark and bitter. This was a cruel, sad, and silent place, with jagged, stony mountains, and whirlwinds that lifted the dust into the scorching air. Smith and his men went on. They followed the Mojave River to its source in the San Bernardino Mountains, which they crossed south of Cajon Pass. On November 27, tired and hungry, their clothes in rags, they reached the San Gabriel Mission.

The Indians and the padres who ran the mission stared at them in amazement. Never before had Americans come to California over the mountains. Father Sánchez, the head of the mission, made them welcome, and they stayed for six weeks.

In California, Smith and his men were foreigners. They had entered Mexican territory without permission and had no right to remain. The Governor refused to let them trap in California or travel through to Oregon.

Padres at San Gabriel welcomed Jedediah Smith when he arrived in California.

Carl S. Dentzel Collection

When beaver became scare in the Rocky Mountains, mountain men went even farther west, blazing trails that at last reached California.

They would have to leave by the same way they had come—and at once.

Smith led his party east through the Cajon Pass. But at the desert they turned north to the San Joaquin Valley. Here they trapped beaver until spring, when they tried to cross the Sierra Nevadas. The wind, the cold, the great drifts of snow, forced them back down the steep side. Smith and two of the men tried again. This time they managed to get over the mountains and the Nevada desert beyond. On July 3, Smith reached his partner's camp at Bear Lake.

Ten days later, he set out again for California with a party of eighteen men. Again he traveled south and west until he came to the villages of the Mojave Indians. As he started across the Colorado River, the Indians suddenly attacked. Ten men were killed; the rest swam to the opposite shore. Their horses were gone, and so were most of their supplies.

All that they had left were five guns, a little ammunition, and fifteen pounds of dried meat. But each man still carried a sharp knife. They hacked out a space for themselves in a cluster of small cottonwood trees, piling up the branches around them. Then they made lances by tieing their knives to the ends of straight branches.

Peering out from the trees, Smith saw four or five hundred Indians slowly creeping toward them. A few of the Indians drew closer, and Smith ordered his two best riflemen to fire. Two Indians fell dead, and the rest ran off. Just before dark, Smith and his band began the long march over desert and mountain. In nine and a half days they were in California.

After getting horses and supplies from Father Sánchez, Smith made his way to the San Joaquin Valley. Here he found the men who had come with him on his first trip. He went on to the San José Mission to get more supplies. He was jailed and sent to Monterey, where the Governor finally agreed to let him go. He journeyed to San Francisco, and then led his trappers north to Oregon. He never returned, but he had explored many unknown places and found the trail to California.

In 1828, while Smith was in Oregon, another party of American trappers arrived in California. They were led by Sylvester Pattie and his son, James Ohio Pattie. For days during their journey they were without water. When their food gave out, they ate their dogs and horses, and the beaver they trapped. At last they crossed the desert into Lower California, only to be arrested and sent under guard to San Diego, where they were jailed.

Prisoners were not treated well in the *calabozo*, as the jail was called. Sylvester Pattie soon became sick and died. James Pattie was set free because of a smallpox epidemic. The Governor learned that he had brought some smallpox vaccine, and named him "Surgeon Extraordinary to his Excellency the Governor of California."

Pattie traveled about California, vaccinating people. Later he claimed that he gave many

*Pushing on through unknown country, the mountain men saw scenes of lakes
and waterfalls and tall trees that no white man had ever seen before.*

Hot, dry deserts, as well as mountains, made the trail to California difficult. Always there was danger of death from thirst or starvation.

hundreds of vaccinations—but Pattie did not always tell the truth. He expected money for what he had done. According to his story, the Governor offered to pay him in land and cattle, and then only if he became a Catholic and a Mexican citizen. Pattie refused. He was so angry with the Governor that he started to join a revolution against him. At last he returned to the United States. He went by way of Mexico, so that he could complain to the government at Mexico City.

Meanwhile, other trappers, both American and Mexican, were on the move toward California. These trappers had their headquarters in New Mexico, in Taos and Santa Fe. They began using the Old Spanish Trail between Santa Fe and Los Angeles, and for years this was an important route to California. Among the New Mexican trappers was Ewing Young, who came to California in 1830. His party of forty included young Kit Carson.

Young made many trips to California, but at last he settled in Oregon. In 1837 he took a trip to San Francisco to buy five or six hundred head of cattle. He drove them to Oregon in a great cattle drive, reaching the Willamette Valley after weary days on the dusty trail.

About four years after Young's first trip to California, Joseph Walker set out from the Great Salt Lake "to steer through an unknown country towards the Pacific." Leading a party of forty to sixty trappers, he crossed the dry, empty land to the Humboldt River. He followed the river, past Humboldt and Carson Sinks, and went on through more deserts. Finally he reached the eastern edge of the Sierra Nevada Mountains, near a lake that was later given his name.

The mountains rose like a wall of rock blocking the way west. The "wind shrieked wild" and the snow was twenty to forty feet deep.

There was "nothing to eat worth mentioning." Even for Walker himself, who was over six feet tall and weighed two hundred pounds, the going was rough. To keep from starving, the men killed some of the horses and ate the meat.

They went on, traveling a few miles every day. The mountains rose steeply from a great valley, which would later be named the Yosemite. There they could see huge domes of rock, and water falling from the awful, steep cliffs in swift waterfalls. Unable to climb down into the deep valley, Walker and his men continued along the ridge. Before coming out of the mountains, they passed giant sequoia trees with trunks a hundred feet around.

Walker and his party fought their way through to the San Joaquin, then went on to San Francisco Bay and the San Juan Bautista Mission. Some of the men decided to stay in California, and in spring Walker formed a new party. In it were fifty-two men, between three and four hundred horses, forty-seven cattle, and a great number of dogs. On the trip back to Salt Lake, Walker discovered a pass through the Sierra mountains—later called Walker Pass —and the Owens Valley.

And so the mountain men went pushing on into the wilderness. They were searching for beaver, for new places to lay their traps—but they showed America the way to California.

Joseph Walker and his party of mountain men were the first Americans to see the Yosemite region. Later, in 1851, the great valley was discovered by Major James D. Savage and Dr. L. H. Bunnell. Dr. Bunnell gave it its name, based on the Miwok Indian word, Uzumati, which means "grizzly bear."

Union Pacific Railroad

ROUTES USED BY
THE SETTLERS

----- Present
state boundaries

0   200
Miles

The Settlers

AMERICANS BEGIN TO ARRIVE IN CALIFORNIA

Beginning in California's earliest days, stories spread about the wonders of the land. Some of the stories stretched the truth. Nowhere in the world was the climate so healthy, the soil so rich, the forests so tall. It was even said that the dew fell every morning on the roses and hardened into a kind of delicious sugar-candy.

The mountain men had their own tales to tell, and among the listeners was John Marsh. A Yankee from Massachusetts, he had been a

student at Harvard University. After graduating, he wandered off to New Mexico and Missouri. But he was still not satisfied, and in 1836 he decided to try his luck in California.

Although he was not a doctor, he got permission from the Mexican officials to practice medicine. Doctors were scarce in California, Marsh did know a little about medicine, and his Harvard diploma proved that he was an educated man. He opened an office in Los

Angeles and took his pay in hides. They brought him enough money to buy land farther north, near Mount Diablo. There he set up a rancho, becoming the first white settler in California's great central valley.

The second white settler was John August Sutter, who had come to America from Switzerland to make his fortune. He landed at New York, and during the next five years he traveled to Missouri, Colorado, New Mexico, Oregon, Hawaii, and Alaska. When he reached California in 1839, he knew that this was where he wanted to stay. He asked the Governor for land, and was granted a huge tract of nearly 50,000 acres near the Sacramento River. He named his land New Helvetia and brought in a large company of men to work for him.

New Helvetia was a colony rather than a rancho, and Sutter was its ruler. He set his men to growing wheat and raising cattle. They also built houses, workshops, a flour mill, a tannery, and a fort with thick adobe walls.

In 1841, Sutter learned that the Russians were giving up Fort Ross and leaving California. He bought everything they owned, including buildings, cattle, horses, mules, sheep, tools, muskets, cannon, and a ship. He returned to New Helvetia on the ship, taking whatever he could with him. He set up twelve of the cannon in his fort, and ordered his vaqueros to Fort Ross to drive down the cattle.

To get their land, both Sutter and Marsh had become Mexican citizens. Even so, they still thought of themselves as Americans, and they wanted more Americans to settle in the valley. Marsh wrote letters about California to his friends in Missouri. The letters were printed in newspapers and read by many people. But it was a mountain man named Antoine Robidoux who started the first big move.

Tired oxen sometimes fell while pulling covered wagons to California.

Carl S. Dentzel Collection

A wagon train in California

A year before Sutter bought Fort Ross, Robidoux talked to a meeting of Missourians in Platte County. He had been to California and seen it for himself—and he liked everything he saw. Truly, it was a country where the spring never ended. Anything would grow there, even oranges. Thousands of wild cattle and horses roamed the hills, and could be caught by anyone. All Californians were friendly—the officials, the rancheros, even the Indians. And the climate was the healthiest on this earth.

"How about the ague?" someone asked. "Any out there?"

Many Missourians suffered from ague, a sickness that caused fever, chills, and shivering. Robidoux answered that there was only one man in California who had ever had a chill.

"It was such a wonder," he said, "that the people of Monterey went eighteen miles into the country to see him shake."

For weeks after the meeting, Platte County buzzed with talk about California. John Bidwell, a young schoolteacher, made up his mind to go west. So did many of his neighbors. Call-

ing themselves the Western Emigration Society, they signed an agreement to set out for California in the spring. Within a month, five hundred people had put down their names.

But, during the winter, they had time to think. The merchants of the county, afraid of losing customers, spoke up against California. Maybe it wasn't such a wonderful place, after all. Besides, getting there would be long and hard and dangerous. People began to say that the whole thing looked like a wild goose chase. In the spring, only sixty-nine persons gathered at Sapling Grove to make the journey. And of them all, only John Bidwell had signed the agreement.

They were not very well prepared. They knew almost nothing about the country they had to cross, except that California lay to the west. They had few maps, and those were poor. They had little money, perhaps no more than a hundred dollars altogether. One man, "Cheyenne" Dawson, could jingle his entire fortune in his pocket—seventy-five cents. They chose John Bartleson captain. He turned out to be as foolish as he was selfish. Bidwell had to take over many of his duties and be the real leader of the company.

Luckily, they were able to travel part of the way with some trappers and missionaries who were going to Oregon. In the party were Thomas Fitzpatrick, a famous mountain man, and Father De Smet, a Catholic missionary. On May 19, 1841, the fourteen wagons and four carts were ready to roll. Whips cracked over the oxen and horses and mules. For better or worse, they were off to California.

Their route was soon to become famous as the Oregon and California Trail. It ran along the Platte River, past the landmarks known as Court House Rocks and Chimney Rock, past the fur trading post of Fort Laramie, then up the Sweetwater River to the Rocky Mountains.

At first, as Bidwell later said, "one day was much like another. We set forth every morning and camped every night...." Then, going up the Platte, they saw so many buffalo that "the plains were black with them for several days' journey as far as the eye could reach." One night the party "had to sit up and fire guns and make what fires we could to keep them from running over us and trampling us into the dust."

One man was killed in an accident; four turned back. The party pushed on up the Rockies, crossing through South Pass. On the western slope, they followed the Bear River to Soda Springs, a "bright and lovely place."

The trappers and missionaries went north, taking the trail to Oregon. Half of the Missouri party went with them. That left Bidwell,

Sutter's Fort, where John Sutter welcomed settlers from the United States

Carl S. Dentzel Collection

Joseph Goldsborough Bruff painted this scene of the north fork of
the Platte River while traveling to California with a wagon train.

Bartleson, and the thirty others still heading for California. The going was so slow that they were afraid the snows would overtake them. They gave up their wagons and packed their supplies on the oxen, horses, and mules. They crossed the desert, killed the oxen for food, and started over the Sierra Nevada mountains.

Now they had to hurry, for already it was late autumn. Snow could fall at any moment, and then they might never see the golden sun of California. But again luck was with them—the snows came late that year. When their food was gone, they killed mules, sometimes eating the meat raw. Weary, half-starved, stumbling over rocks, they went on.

Bidwell began to think they would never get beyond the fearful mountains. Then, on October 30, he was able to write in his journal: "We had gone about three miles this morning, when lo! to our great delight we beheld a wide valley!..." The next day, he added: "Joyful sight...Hundreds of antelope in view! Elk tracks thousands! killed two antelopes and some wild fowls..." And on October 31, they were camped in the valley, which was covered with young grass, like a field of wheat in May.

Several days later, they met a half-naked Indian horseman. He brought them to John Marsh's rancho. Marsh was helpful—but he made them pay for his help. Bidwell thought he was "the meanest man in California." Some of the Missourians, including Bidwell, went to New Helvetia. They were welcomed by John Sutter. The rest settled in various places.

A few weeks later, another party arrived in Los Angeles from Santa Fe. No settlers arrived in 1842, but in 1843 two large parties reached California safely. A Californian who saw one of the parties at New Helvetia wrote to a friend: "You see how immigration progresses and the Yankees will not be stopped unless by the Pacific Ocean."

Each year, more Americans settled in California. They wrote letters home, and everywhere in the United States there was talk about the wonderful land in the west. Newspapers and magazines printed report after report, and called for more settlers.

In 1846, the Donner party was trapped in the mountains by an unusually early winter. A howling wind piled the snow into drifts ten feet high. Of the seventy-nine men, women and children in the party, thirty-four died of cold and starvation.

But by that time there were enough settlers to change the flag that flew over California.

During the long journey west, settlers sometimes were attacked by Indians.

American settlers who wanted their own government made the first Bear Flag.

The Bear Flag Republic

THE AMERICANS REVOLT AGAINST MEXICAN RULE

Commodore Thomas Ap Catesby Jones, of the United States Navy, was puzzled. Standing on the deck of his ship, he looked around at the bay of Monterey. All he could see on the blue water was his own two ships, the frigate *United States* and the sloop *Cyane*.

As commander of the Pacific squadron of five ships, Jones had been cruising the Pacific Ocean. When he reached Peru, he was given a message. Something in it made him believe that the United States and Mexico were at war. He also believed that Mexico was about to give California to England. Quickly he sailed to Monterey with two of his ships, and on October 19, 1842, he came into the harbor.

Jones looked around again, then stared at the land through a telescope. Why was there no cannon fire from the presidio? Still puzzled, he ordered an armed party of his men to go ashore. They found most of the soldiers in the fields, working peacefully under the warm sun. The presidio itself badly needed repairs, and the cannons looked as though they could not be fired. The commandante of the presidio was even more puzzled than Jones. He knew of no war. He had heard of no war. There *was* no war.

Commodore Jones decided not to take any chances. He demanded the surrender of the presidio and the town, took down the Mexican flag, and ran up the American flag in its place. A day or two passed, and Jones saw that he had made a mistake. Truly, there was no war. He returned Monterey to its Mexican officials, put up the Mexican flag again, and apologized. He went to Los Angeles and apologized to the Governor, who gave a ball for him. And, after the dancing, the singing, the feasting, and the drinking of wine, he sailed away.

Jones' mistake was really not so surprising. Americans wanted their country to grow until it stretched from coast to coast, and for some time they had been keeping an eye on California. And they were afraid that a strong nation like England might send ships and simply take the rich land. The United States Government made several offers to buy California, or at least part of it. Mexico refused to sell.

But all the while settlers were moving across the border, and Americans felt that sooner or later, one way or another, California would join the United States. Only a year before Jones came to Monterey, a U.S. Navy exploring expedition, led by Lieutenant Charles Wilkes, had visited California. Wilkes reported that San Francisco was one of the finest ports in the world and that California could easily be taken from Mexico.

In 1844, another exploring expedition came to California. This one was led by an army officer, John C. Frémont. His guides were Kit Carson and Thomas Fitzpatrick, both famous mountain men. The expedition first traveled to Oregon by the Oregon Trail, then turned to the Southeast, going east of the Cascade and Sierra Nevada Mountains. Frémont suddenly decided to go west over the Sierras to California—something no white man had ever done in winter.

It was already January, and the Indians warned that this was a season of death in the Sierras. But Frémont's mind was made up, and he ordered his men to start up the steep slope. For days they pushed on among the jagged peaks. As Frémont wrote later, around them was only "rock upon rock—rock upon rock— snow upon snow—snow upon snow."

To keep alive, they ate mule meat and even dog meat. There seemed to be no way out; they seemed imprisoned in the icy mountains. But Carson knew that the Sacramento Valley lay below, and at last he found a pass. Coming down into the valley, they made their way to Sutter's Fort. Sutter welcomed them and helped them get supplies and fresh horses. After a few weeks' rest they started back, using the Old Spanish Trail.

Frémont went on to Washington and made a report to the Government. It included the best maps yet made of the West. The report was printed as a book, and thousands of Americans read of his adventures. They read, too, of California's wonders, such as the great green valley, blazing with wild flowers, where huge herds of wild horses, elk, deer, and antelope wandered through the tall grass.

By 1845, Frémont was again on his way west. In December he was in California with an expedition of sixty well-armed men. General José Castro, the military commander of California, gave them permission to spend the winter if they kept away from the seacoast.

For several weeks Frémont camped near San José. Then he started southwest. On March 3, 1846, he made camp in the Salinas Valley. General Castro knew that the Mexican Government was worried about losing its lands to the United States. Only last July it had forbidden any more Americans from settling in California. And now here was a well-armed party of Americans hardly more than twenty-five miles from the town of Monterey. Were they planning an attack? If they were, it was up to him to stop them. He ordered Frémont and his men to leave at once.

Instead, Frémont marched his men to a hill called Hawk's Peak. Acting as though he were already at war, he built breastworks and raised the American flag. Castro got together some Mexican soldiers and again ordered Frémont to leave. After three days, Frémont took down the flag and began to move slowly toward the north.

At Klamath Lake, near the border between California and Oregon, a man came riding into Frémont's camp with news. An official messenger sent by the United States Government had been trailing Frémont and was not far behind. He was Lieutenant Archibald H. Gillespie of the United States Marine Corps, and he gave Frémont letters and dispatches

U.S. Navy ships which patrolled the Pacific at the time of the Mexican War

from Washington. Frémont never told anyone what messages they carried—but he went no farther north.

That night, Frémont was so busy thinking about the messages that he forgot to place guards around the camp. Just before morning, a shout rang out in the darkness. Indians were attacking the camp. One man's skull had already been split by a tomahawk; another man lay groaning and gasping. After a fierce fight, the Indians were driven off. In the morning light, Frémont counted the dead—three of his party and the chief of the Indians. He ordered his men to break camp, and soon they were on the move. They stopped long enough to set fire to an Indian village and kill fourteen Indians. Then they kept going south until they reached Marysville Buttes, in the Sacramento Valley.

There were American settlers living in the valley, and they were tired of being ruled by Mexico. They came running to Frémont with all kinds of talk—talk they had heard from their neighbors:

"I hear they're goin' to run us out o' Californy! Castro's raisin' soldiers to do it!"

"And they say the Mexicans are rousin' up the Indians to massacre us! We've got to stop it!"

On June 10 the settlers did more than talk. A small band of them captured some horses that had been rounded up for General Castro. Four days later, a larger band of thirty-three men came tramping into the little town of Sonoma. They took several prisoners, among them Mariano Guadalupe Vallejo.

It happened that Vallejo was friendly to Americans and wanted California to join the United States. That made no difference to the rough settlers in their leather hunting shirts. Vallejo was an important leader in northern California. Taking him prisoner would show that they meant business. For the settlers were out to overthrow the Mexican Government and set up their own—the California Republic.

Every republic needs a flag, and the settlers quickly made one. On a large piece of white cloth they painted a grizzly bear and a star. Under the bear and the star they painted the words "California Republic" in large letters. Shouting and cheering, they raised the flag in the plaza, or public square, of Sonoma. The

Los Angeles County Museum—Modern Enterprises

After American sailors and Marines captured Monterey, they started to raise the flag. The rope jammed, and a midshipman ran forward and climbed the pole. Freeing the flag, he shouted, "Hoist away!" This time the flag rose to the top, signalling the end of Mexican rule.

Bear Flaggers were now ready to fight for independence against the Californians.

They were soon joined by Frémont and his men. Frémont took charge, and more settlers came to fight under his command. Two Americans and a few Californians were killed; other Californians were captured and held prisoner.

Then, on July 10, a messenger came riding up to Frémont. This time the message was not kept secret. Fighting between the United States and Mexico had started in Texas on May 8. American warships were already in the bay of Monterey. A force of sailors and marines had taken the town and declared that California was now part of the United States.

The Bear Flaggers hauled down their flag, raised the flag of the United States, and that was the end of the Bear Flag Republic. It had lasted less than a month.

The taking of Monterey, painted by U.S. Navy gunner Myers in a letter

Bancroft Library

Under fire of "The Old Woman's Gun," the Americans retreated at San Pedro.

California Becomes American

THE UNITED STATES WINS THE MEXICAN WAR

There was war in California, but at first it was a strange war, without battles or bloodshed. On July 7, Commodore John D. Sloat of the United States Navy took Monterey, and not a shot was fired. Soon the American flag was also flying over San Francisco, Sonoma, and Sutter's Fort—and still not a shot was fired.

On July 15, Commodore Robert F. Stockton became commander of the Americans. He made Frémont a major in charge of the Bear Flaggers, who joined the United States Army as volunteers. Stockton took San Pedro; Frémont took San Diego. And still not a shot was fired. Governor Pio Pico and General José Castro escaped to Mexico, and their soldiers simply went home. The Americans could find no enemy to fight.

On August 13, Stockton and Frémont marched into Los Angeles. Ahead of them stepped a band, playing *Hail Columbia* and *Yankee Doodle*. Behind them came Stockton's sailors and marines in their blue uniforms, and Frémont's Bear Flaggers in buckskins. Last of all came carts pulled by oxen, carrying guns, ammunition, and supplies. The Angelenos, as the people of Los Angeles were called, stayed in their houses. Not that they were afraid. But who knew what the Americans might do?

As the sun went down, Stockton looked around at the quiet, dusty streets. And then he had an idea. He ordered the band to give a concert in the Plaza. Never before had a real band played in Los Angeles, and the Angelenos loved music. The loud singing of trumpets and trombones, the whistling of flutes, the crash of drums, called them out of their homes. They crowded around the bandsmen, shouting, "*Viva! Viva!*"

For two weeks, Stockton and Frémont stayed in Los Angeles. The band played again; the Angelenos cheered. Stockton and Frémont then went to Monterey. As far as they could see, the war was over. Stockton sent Kit Carson traveling eastward to Washington with a message for President Polk. The message said that all of California was in American hands.

At San Pascual, Californians fought Americans with long Spanish lances.

But Stockton had left fifty soldiers in Los Angeles, under the command of Archibald Gillespie. And Gillespie was a man who liked to give orders and make rules. Angelenos were not allowed to walk the streets unless they were alone. They were forbidden to gather together, even in their own homes. They could not ride their horses through town faster than a trot. Shops had to be closed before evening. Many persons were arrested, often for no reason at all.

The Angelenos did not seem to care much whether they were governed by Mexico or the United States. But they hated to be ordered about, and more than once they had made trouble for their Mexican officials. They could make trouble for Gillespie, too. On September 23, led by José María Flores, they rose up against the Americans.

Gillespie and his fifty soldiers were driven to Fort Hill, in back of the church above the Plaza. Surrounded and outnumbered, they badly needed help. They could get it only from Commodore Stockton at Monterey, four hun-

dred miles away. One man volunteered to carry a message to Stockton. He was John Brown, an American trapper known as Juan Flaco, or Lean John.

That night Gillespie scribbled these words on a cigarette paper: "Believe the bearer." Lean John Brown hid the paper in his long hair and rode off. He broke through the Californians' lines, then heard hoofbeats pounding through the darkness. The Californians had seen him and were chasing him. There was a burst of gunfire and his horse, frightened, leaped over a gulch. Looking back, Lean John saw that the gulch was thirteen feet wide and the Californians' horses would not jump it. He rode on for about two miles, when suddenly his horse dropped dead. A small hole in its flank showed that it had been hit by a bullet.

By the light of the moon, Lean John walked and ran twenty-seven miles to a ranch. He talked the ranchero into giving him a horse, and went on. Day and night he rode, picking up fresh horses wherever he could, until he reached Monterey. There he was told that

Stockton had gone to San Francisco. After a few hours' sleep, he rode to San Francisco and delivered his message. In five days he had traveled nearly five hundred miles.

Meanwhile, Gillespie was forced to surrender. Flores, the leader of the Californians, did not know what to do with the Americans. He did not want to kill them, and he had no place to jail them. He decided to let them go to San Pedro, if they would sail away on the first ship to leave port. Gillespie agreed, and with drums beating, flags flying, his men marched to San Pedro.

While they were waiting for their ship to sail, another ship, the *Savannah*, came into the harbor. Aboard her were several hundred Americans, sent by Stockton after he had seen Lean John Brown. With more than three hundred men under his command, Gillespie changed his mind about sailing away. Instead, he would attack Los Angeles.

The day the men began their march was furiously hot. As they tramped across the dry fields, they seemed to be breathing dust rather than air. Often they had to push through great thickets of mustard grass taller than their tallest man. Tired, dirty, aching with thirst, they pitched camp on the Domínguez Rancho long before evening.

The next morning they started marching again. At a little distance from Los Angeles, a force of Californians came charging at them on horseback. Some of the Californians carried rifles. Others carried lances they had made by fastening a sharp metal blade to the end of an eight-foot willow pole. And they had the Old Woman's Gun—a small cannon which an old woman had hidden when the Americans had taken Los Angeles.

Now the cannon was mounted on two wheels and an axle. One of the Californians fired it by touching off the powder charge with a lighted cigarette. The Americans scattered to escape the cannon ball. The Californians scattered, too, for the Old Woman's Gun had a bad recoil.

As the Americans rushed forward to capture the cannon, the Californians lassoed it with reatas, quickly pulled it away, loaded and fired. Again and again this happened, and after two days the Americans retreated. They reached San Pedro with four dead or dying, and six badly wounded to care for.

But other Americans were marching toward Los Angeles. Colonel Stephen W. Kearny had set out from Santa Fe for California with three hundred troops. On the way, he met Kit Carson, who was carrying Stockton's message to

On the bank of the San Gabriel River, the Americans drove back the Californians.

Washington. Kearny read the message, which said that all California was in American hands. He sent two hundred of his soldiers back to Sante Fe and told Carson to stay with him as a guide.

The trip across the Colorado desert left Kearny's men worn and weary. They were given no time to rest. For, near the little village of San Pascual, Andres Pico and a hundred hard-riding Californians swooped down on them. Eighteen Americans were killed and many more wounded in the worst battle of the California fighting. During the next few days several volunteers, including Carson and another mountain man named Alex Godey, broke through the enemy lines. Crawling over rock and cactus, they reached San Diego, where they asked Stockton for help. He sent 180 men who helped Kearny's ragged troops get safely to San Diego.

After several weeks, Kearny and Stockton were ready to lead their six hundred men north against Los Angeles. By January 8, they were at the San Gabriel River. On the heights of the opposite bank, Flores and his Californians were waiting. There were as many of

them as there were Americans, but the leaders had quarreled and their gunpowder was poor. The Americans crossed the river and pushed the Californians back. There was a little more fighting the next day. Then Flores gave up, turned his command over to Andres Pico, and ran off to Mexico. On January 10, the Americans raised their flag over Los Angeles.

At the same time, Frémont was marching south from Monterey with four hundred soldiers, settlers, and trappers. A settler warned him that the Californians had set a trap for him near Gaviota, north of Santa Barbara. He took his men through San Marcos Pass to Santa Barbara. From there he went through the Santa Clara Valley towards San Fernando.

Pico saw that any more fighting would be useless. He surrendered, and on January 13, 1847, in an adobe house near Cahuenga Pass, he signed a surrender agreement. Frémont asked only that the Californians give up some of their arms and obey the law of the United States.

The Californians had been Spanish, then Mexican; from now on they would be Americans and live still a different kind of life.

Myers' picture shows billows of smoke rising at La Mesa on the Los Angeles River. But the actual fighting, which took place on January 9, 1847, was soon over. The next day the Americans marched into Los Angeles.

Franklin D. Roosevelt Library

The gold that started the Gold Rush came from the ditch of Sutter's sawmill.

Gold from the American River!

THE DISCOVERY AT SUTTER'S MILL

Rain fell from the dark January sky, beating against the roofs of Fort Sutter. Even in his office, John Sutter could feel the chill of the damp air. And yet, he was not unhappy. This gray day would pass, and the sun would come out again. Besides, things were going well for him. He was getting good crops from his fields and orchards; his herds of cattle and flocks of sheep were growing larger.

He smiled as he thought of how California was changing. The Mexican War was over, and an American military governor ruled the land. Soon a peace treaty would be signed, officially making California a part of the United States. More settlers than ever would be coming across the mountains—and more settlers meant more business, more profits, more money.

That was why he had hired men to build a sawmill, on the American River in the Coloma Valley. Using waterpower, the mill would saw logs into lumber. The new settlers would buy the lumber for houses.

Sutter was still thinking about the settlers when there was a noise at the door. A bearded man, soaked with rain, was walking into the office. He was James W. Marshall, the carpenter in charge of building the sawmill. Sutter looked up at him, wondering why he had come in such weather. Marshall said that he had important news. Could they go someplace where they would be alone?

Nodding, Sutter led the way to the rooms in which he lived. After the door had been closed, Marshall took a rag from his pocket. Wrapped in the rag were some bits and flakes of shining metal. Marshall had found them on January 24, in the tailrace—the ditch that carried away the water—of the sawmill.

Sutter's Mill and the Coloma Valley, as they looked in 1851

While the rain fell on the roof with the sound of drumbeats, the two men stared at the metal and at each other. Then Sutter picked up an encyclopedia and read the article on gold. He and Marshall poured acid on samples of the shining metal, weighed it, and made every other test they could.

Although the rain was still pouring down, Marshall refused to stay. He hurried back to the sawmill, to Coloma, to the hidden treasure of gold. Sutter tried not to seem excited. But he slept little that night, and a few days later he went to Coloma himself. The men working on the sawmill showed him the gold dust and flakes they had collected. It was true, then— there was a treasure in this earth.

Pushing his cane into the ground, Sutter said, "By Jo, it is rich!"

He tried to keep the discovery a secret, but it was impossible. Passed on from one person to another, the news spread. By March, just

when the sawmill was ready to turn out lumber, most of the men there left to hunt for gold. At Sutter's Fort, as Sutter wrote later, everybody left "from the clerk to the cook." Two thousand hides rotted in the tannery; forty thousand bushels of wheat were never threshed. "The same thing happened," Sutter wrote, "in every branch of business which I carried on at the time."

In May, Samuel Brannan, a newspaper owner and merchant from San Francisco, visited Coloma to see what was going on. A few days before the end of the month, he was back in San Francisco. Riding into the plaza, he held up a small bottle filled with gold dust.

"Gold!" he shouted. "Gold! Gold from the American River!"

The words rang through the town like a bell rousing up the people. *Gold! Gold! Gold from the American River!* Men who had been satisfied to farm, or tend shop, or teach school, or bake bread, forgot about their work. Their eyes burned with a new kind of fever—gold fever. They dreamed of piles of gold, of heaps of money, of mansions and huge marble castles, of servants bowing and scurrying off to carry out their slightest wish. . . .

And so they set off for the American River, for Coloma, the valley where wealth could be scooped up from the ground. Some went by boat. Others went on horseback, on wagons, and on foot. Before the end of June, more than half of San Francisco's eight hundred people had gone hunting for gold. Sailors left their ships in the harbor and ran off to join the search. The town seemed empty. The alcalde, or mayor, closed his office. The two weekly newspapers closed, too. In its last issue, one of them, the *Californian,* said:

"The whole country from San Francisco to Los Angeles, and from the sea shore to the base of the Sierra Nevadas, resounds to the sordid cry of *gold!* GOLD!! GOLD!!! while the field is left half planted, the house half built, and everything neglected but the manufacture of shovels and pickaxes. . . ."

The *Californian* was right. The news was spreading—to Monterey, to San José, to Santa Barbara, to Los Angeles. In Monterey, almost all the men ran off to the gold fields. Only women, a gang of prisoners, and a few soldiers remained in town. And even the soldiers were running off, one by one. Their pay was seven dollars a month, and every day they heard stories of gold strikes, of miners who had "struck it rich."

Five men working together were said to have made $75,000 in three months. A miner working alone was reported to have made $50,000 in a few weeks. Other men said they were making sixty dollars a day, a hundred, a thousand, two thousand. Probably most made around twenty dollars a day, which was still much more than they could have earned back home.

The news reached Hawaii in June, and a number of men set out from Honolulu. Ships from Hawaii brought the news to Oregon, where American settlers started for California on horseback and in covered wagons. From Mexico, too, and Peru and Chile came the

With pickaxes, shovels, and tin pans, gold seekers hoped to find a fortune.

gold seekers. By the end of 1848 there were at least five thousand miners actually at work in the gold fields, and several thousand more on the way.

With a shovel and a pickaxe, or just a knife and a horn spoon, they dug the precious metal from the ground. Along rivers and streams, they "panned" for gold. First they scooped up water, sand, and gravel in a tin pan. Swirling the water around, they spilled it out, washing out some of the sand and gravel with it. They did this again and again, adding more water each time. The gold, which was heavier than sand or gravel, settled to the bottom of the pan.

But panning was hard work and slow work. To speed the job, some miners used a "cradle" or "rocker." This was an oblong box on rockers, something like a baby's cradle. A sieve at the top of the box screened out the large rocks. Particles of gold, sand, gravel, and water fell through the sieve. The gold was caught by cleats nailed across the bottom of the box.

Every miner looked for "color"—traces of gold in the gravel. If a miner found "pay dirt," which was gravel with traces of gold, he "staked out a claim." That meant getting the right to work a particular piece of land. To mark the land, he put up a post or a pile of rocks with his name on it. He then had his claim recorded in a book kept by the miners in that "district." As long as he worked his claim, all other miners had to keep off. A dishonest miner who tried to work a claim that was not his own was called a "claim jumper."

Merchants followed the miners to the gold fields. They set up shop in tents and shacks, selling such things as food, clothing, whiskey,

The miner at left is "panning," while his companion uses a "cradle."
The third miner is crushing ore with a rock attached to a handle.

Tree'd

Nooning

shovels, pickaxes, and pans. Prices were high. Flour sold for as much as eighteen dollars a barrel. A shirt might sell for sixteen dollars. In one town, breakfast for two men, of sardines, cheese, bread, butter, and two bottles of ale, was forty-three dollars.

The miners grumbled, but they paid. They knew that hauling in goods of any kind was expensive. Besides, what did prices matter when a man could get rich overnight? Tomorrow a "lucky strike" might fill his "poke"—the little bag in which miners kept their gold—with gold dust and nuggets.

In 1848 it seemed as if there would be no end to the gold, and slowly the news spread to the eastern part of the United States. On December 5, speaking to Congress, President Polk told of the discovery of gold on the nation's new lands. Two days later, a Naval officer arrived in Washington with a tea box containing $3,000 worth of gold. The gold was put on display, and suddenly there was an explosion of talk about California. Soon after the new year, men from every state in the Union were setting out for the gold fields. Forty-Niners, they were called, because the year was 1849. The gold rush was on.

Slap Jacks

These four drawings show scenes from the gold miner's life in the Sierra Nevada Mountains.

Rush for new Diggings

Henry E. Huntington Library

THE WAY THEY GO TO CALIFORNIA.

There were no rockets or air lines in 1849, but the artist used his imagination to show how anxious the gold seekers were to reach California.

The Gold Rush

MINERS SEEK FORTUNES IN THE GOLD FIELDS

The news about gold in California seemed to roar across the country and around the world. Preachers preached about it. Writers wrote about it. Everybody talked about it. And thousands of men—good men, bad men; young men, and men who were not so young; educated men, and men who could not write their own names; men who wanted adventure, men who wanted to change their lives, men who wanted a little money for their families, men who wanted to make a fortune overnight—all had the same thought. California, that's the land for me! See you at Sutter's Fort! Better get there before the gold gives out! Better hurry! Rush!

But California was a long way off, and getting there was not easy. Many gold seekers on the east coast decided to go by sea. They tramped the waterfront streets of Boston, New York, and other port cities, looking for a ship. They jammed the ticket offices. They pushed into clothing stores to buy miner's clothes—flannel shirts, loose coats, broad felt hats, and high boots. They bought supplies at shops that advertised: California Goods—Recommended to Gentlemen about Starting for California . . . Tents and Camping Equipment. . . Shovels. . . Hatchets and Axes . . . Bowie Knives . . . Six Barrelled Revolvers . . . Money Belts specially made for Gold. . . .

"Get 'em now, boys," said the shopkeepers. "You'll need 'em. Nothing like this in California."

They boarded the ships, singing:

Oh, California!
That's the land for me!
I'm bound for Californy
With my washbowl on my knee!

Yes, they were bound for California, around South America, around Cape Horn, and north to San Francisco. They sailed from 17,000 to 18,000 miles. The ships were crowded. The food was poor. The sea was often stormy. Even so, it was the safest and most comfortable way to go. But it cost several hundred dollars, and took from four to eight months.

Some gold-seekers traveled by steamship to the Isthmus of Panama. They went up the Chagres River in small boats, and crossed the land on mules. Then they went north by steamship. This sea-and-land trip might take as little as thirty-three to thirty-five days, if all went well. But it cost at least $400 first-class, and there was always the danger of fever in the hot, damp jungle.

Altogether, perhaps 40,000 of the Forty-Niners reached California by sea and by the sea-and-land route. Just as many gold-seekers came by land. Loading up their covered wagons, they set off along the trails broken by Frémont and the mountain men. Wagon after wagon creaked westward, their wheels leaving deep ruts in the ground.

There was little trouble from Indians. But there was blazing heat and freezing cold, thirst and hunger and sickness. To lighten their wagons, the gold-seekers threw out heavy chests, bedsteads, anything they could do without. One Forty-Niner wrote that in the desert "I passed the carcases of 1200 head of cattle and horses and a great many wagons—Harnesses—cooking utensils—tools water casks &c.&c. . . . We also see many men on the point of starvation begging for bread."

A Forty-Niner bound for San Francisco by ship painted this picture in his journal as he set out from Newbury Port, Massachusetts.

Henry E. Huntington Library

One party of gold seekers became lost in the desert and were not rescued for twenty-six days. Starting off again, one of the party said, "Goodbye, Death Valley!" In this way the desert got its name.

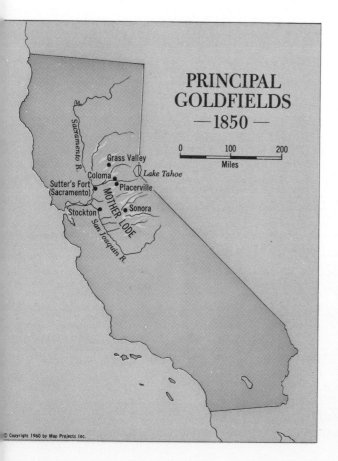

PRINCIPAL
GOLDFIELDS
— 1850 —

0   100   200
Miles

Sacramento R.

Grass Valley
Coloma   Lake Tahoe
Sutter's Fort   Placerville
(Sacramento)
MOTHER LODE
Stockton   Sonora
San Joaquin R.

Hundreds of the Forty-Niners died. Others barely escaped death. One party, trying a short cut, came to a deep, desert valley—a wild, fearful, dreary place of "dreadful sands and shadows . . ."

Two men of the party, Manly and Rogers, rode off for help. Returning with food twenty-six days later, they saw the body of a man lying "on his back with arms extended wide, and his little canteen, made of two powder flasks, lying by his side empty."

They saw the wagons, too, but no people. Nothing moved. Nothing made a sound. To break the awful quiet, Manly fired his gun. "As if by magic," he wrote later, "a man came from under a wagon. . . . He threw up his arms high over his head and shouted, 'The boys have come! The boys have come!'" Then the other people in the party came out of the wagons, several of them throwing their arms around Manly and Rogers.

Some weeks later, they all started off again. As they climbed up the Panamint Mountains, they looked back at the desert, silent under the sun. "Good-bye," they said. "Good-bye, Death Valley" And Death Valley was the name of the desert from that day on.

And still the Forty-Niners came, pouring into California. They came from every one of the thirty states, and from Europe and Asia and Australia. The population of California grew from about 14,000 in 1848 to 223,000 in 1852. Before the Gold Rush, San Francisco was a village of 812 persons. By 1852, it was a city with a population of more than 30,000.

As long as they lived, the Forty-Niners would remember the hardships of the trail. But they would remember, too, the great, green prairies in the spring, the songs around the campfire, the mountains against the setting sun. And at the end of the trail lay California—and gold.

Gold, gold, gold . . . and with the honest men came dishonest men, to snatch their share of the wealth. Bandits like Joaquín Murrieta roamed the highways, holding up travelers,

and they did not mind killing to get their loot. In the gold fields themselves, as one miner wrote, were vagabonds, scoundrels, rascals, pickpockets, thieves, and gamblers from everywhere in the world. The mining camps were too new to have laws or judges or courts, so the miners often handled criminals in their own way. They chose juries, held trials, and gave swift punishment. Thieves and murderers were flogged, ordered to move on, or hanged from a tree.

Altogether, the miners lived a hard, rough life. They slept in tents and shacks. They cooked their food—mostly beans, salt pork, beef, coffee, bread—over open fires. For amusement, they drank or gambled or danced. Women were scarce, and the miners danced with one another to the music of fiddles and banjos. And sometimes dancers and singers came to the gold fields and put on shows.

Sunday was a day of rest—at least, it was a day of rest from mining. The miners washed

The way west was long and hard, and sometimes death ended the journey.

Henry E. Huntington Library

On the sea-and-land route to California, travelers rode mules through the jungle of Panama. T. G. Bruff drew this sketch in Panama in 1851.

and mended their clothes. They repaired their tools. They made bread by frying dough in iron pans. If a traveling preacher visited the camp, they could attend church services. More often, they made their way to the nearest town, to shop, to pick up mail, to gamble, and to drink.

Each year, gold became harder to find. Some lucky miners did strike it rich. The rest went on searching, digging, panning—and moving. When they heard of a new place where gold had been found, they raced to stake out a claim. New camps and towns sprang up in a day—Red Gulch, Skunk Gulch, Shirt Tail Canyon, You Bet, Hangtown, Git-Up-and-Git. Some of the towns were deserted after the gold gave out and became "ghost towns." Others grew and changed their names.

By 1850, few miners were making more than ten dollars a day, and many were making less. To get gold now, they had to use real engineering, and that meant working in groups. They dammed and turned aside rivers to reach the gold that lay in holes and cracks beneath the water. They built "long toms," which were much like large cradles. They added sluices—troughs with cleats on the bottoms to catch the particles of gold. They needed water for the toms and sluices, and they dug ditches to bring in water from lakes and streams.

Another method of getting gold was hydraulic mining. With water sprayed through a hose or pipe, the miners washed down whole hillsides of gravel. The most difficult method of all was vein or quartz mining. The miners tunneled into mountains with picks and explosives, digging out the ore from the solid rock.

The days when a man could pick up a fortune with his own hands were over. Mining was becoming an industry, with large companies organized by business men. Some of the miners went back home, disgusted and disappointed. Some became wanderers. The rest stayed in California, to work small claims, to

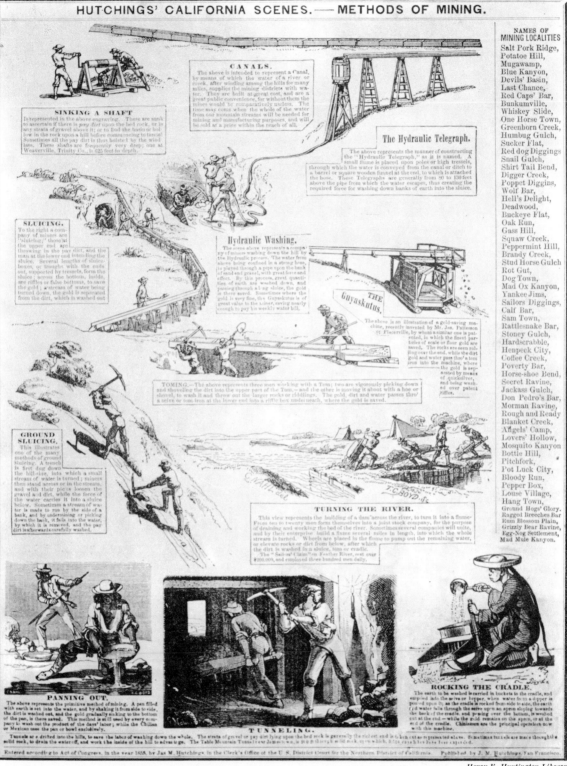

On a page of a California magazine published in the 1850's are shown different ways of mining for gold. At the right is a list of the strange names given to mining towns.

Title Insurance and Trust Co., Los Angeles

*A photograph of busy San Francisco during the Gold
Rush, taken at Montgomery and Commercial Streets*

*James W. Marshall was the first man to find
gold at Sutter's sawmill, but it never made him
rich. Claim-jumpers pushed him off his land,
and the law was no help. Judge and jury were
friends of the men who had taken his land, and
decided against him. At one time, to make a little
money, he sold cards with his autograph, like
the one below. He died a poor man, in 1885.*

Carl S. Dentzel Collection

AUTOGRAPH OF

OLD SUTTER MILL

Jas. W. Marshall

THE DISCOVERER OF GOLD IN CALIFORNIA

January 19th, 1848.

take jobs with the large mining companies,
to farm, and to work in shops.

Perhaps the greatest disappointment came
to the two men who had started the Gold
Rush, Marshall and Sutter. After his first discovery, Marshall seemed to have no luck at
finding gold, and to make a living he took a
job in a blacksmith shop.

Sutter saw his fields overrun by gold-seekers
and squatters, who claimed the land as their
own and refused to move. He spent years trying to prove that the land was really his. At
last, he gave up. He moved east, far from
New Helvetia, to a little town in Pennsylva-
nia. There he lived out his days on a small
pension from the state of California, an old
and ruined man.

Los Angeles in 1857 was still an adobe village. Main Street is at the left; Los Angeles Street, where many merchants had shops, is at the right.

Years of Change

LIFE IN THE NEW STATE

The Gold Rush began the years of change, change in the land and in the lives of those who lived on it. The change was swift, but not swift enough for the impatient Californians. They wanted California made a state, with its own laws and government. As a start, they elected forty-eight delegates to draw up a constitution, or set of laws.

Early in September, 1849, the forty-eight men met at the schoolhouse in the sunny little town of Monterey. They had many questions to decide. All the United States wondered whether California would allow slavery or be a free state. The delegates quickly agreed that California should be free. Within six weeks, they completed their work of drafting a constitution.

In November, the people of California voted in favor of the new constitution and elected a governor and a legislature. The legislature, in turn, chose two United States senators. The senators traveled to Washington, where they asked Congress to make California a state. Again slavery was the most important question, and Congress discussed it for months.

Almost a year went by, and no word reached California from Washington. Then, in October of 1850, the mailship *Oregon* came steaming into San Francisco Bay. Flags flew from all her masts, and the boom of her cannon echoed from the city's hills. This meant that she carried news, big news, and people hurried down to the wharf. They learned that on September 9 Congress had voted to admit California

When California became a state, San Franciscans held a grand celebration.

as a free state. A cheer rose from the crowd, and men ran through the streets, whooping and yelling and shouting:

"We're in the Union! We're in the Union! California is a state!"

Guns were fired into the air. Bells rang. Even strangers shook hands and pounded each other on the back. Stagecoaches and riders on horseback spread the news to other towns. From one end of the new state to the other, Californians celebrated. At night, they lit huge bonfires. They danced and paraded and listened to speeches. They waved flags that were already out of date—flags with only thirty stars. Now another star would be added for California, the thirty-first state.

The new state had its own laws, but they were not always obeyed. San Francisco, with dozens of saloons and gambling places, was a roaring, restless, lawless town. Officials either did not know what to do about it, or were dishonest themselves. Robbery, murder, and other crimes went unpunished.

Once more there were impatient Californians who wanted a change. In 1851, a group of San Franciscans formed the first Vigilance Committee. Like the miners in the gold camps, they took their own prisoners, held their own trials, and dealt out punishment. They hanged three men, whipped one, and forced twenty-eight to leave the city.

For a while, things were better, and the Vigilance Committee disbanded. But by 1855 crime was worse than ever, and even murderers often went free. James King, a newspaper editor, wrote that politicians, business men, and criminals were all working together to break the law. His newspaper, the *Daily Evening Bulletin,* printed the names of the lawbreakers — and among them was James P. Casey, a county official.

One evening, Casey waited outside the newspaper office, a pistol in his hand. As soon as he saw King coming through the door, he fired. King fell to the ground, shot, and died a few days later.

FORT VIGILANT

The San Francisco Vigilantes carefully guarded their headquarters.

Casey was locked up in the city jail. But many San Franciscans were afraid that he would be freed by dishonest officials. Some of the most respected men in the city quickly formed the Second Vigilance Committee. They enlisted several thousand men, arming and drilling them like a small army. Three days later, on a Sunday morning, the Vigilantes were ready to act. On foot or on horseback, they marched toward the jail, carrying rifles and pistols. Crowds, as silent as the armed men, gathered on the streets to watch them. The only sound was the tramp and shuffle of marching feet, and the thud of horses' hoofs.

At the jail, the Vigilantes placed guards around the building. They aimed a small cannon at the iron door, and handed in a note to the jailer. He let them take Casey, who was hustled into a carriage and hauled off to the Vigilantes' headquarters. An hour later, they took another man from the jail. He was Charles Cora, the murderer of a United States marshal. The Vigilantes held a trial for the two

prisoners and found them guilty. On Thursday, just as King's funeral began, Casey and Cora were hanged.

After that, the Vigilantes made their own arrests. Some of the criminals were turned over to the regular officers and went on trial before regular courts. Some, including a judge, were ordered to leave the city.

In other towns, in other parts of California, vigilance committees were also formed. Many were no better than lynch mobs. A Los Angeles man who was hanged was later proved to have been innocent. A Los Angeles mayor resigned, took charge of a hanging, and was then re-elected. A complete story of this same hanging was printed in a newspaper hours before it actually happened. During 1854 and 1855, twenty-two men were hanged by Vigilantes. The hangings went on into the 1860's, until better officials were elected and Californians learned to leave criminals to the law.

Years of change ... and in southern California they began with the "Great Boom." No

Forty-Niners came here, for this was cattle country, and the gold fields were miles away. In 1850, all of Los Angeles County had only 3,500 people. The rancheros still lived in their adobe houses, with their big families and servants and vaqueros, just as they had under Mexican rule. But the Forty-Niners had to eat, and they wanted beef. Northward, up the trails from the ranchos, vaqueros drove huge herds of steers, which sold for fifty to a hundred dollars a head.

Never had there been such a market for cattle, and never had the rancheros seen so much money. They liked living well, and now they could afford it. They bought rugs for the earth floors of their houses, golden spurs for

A California vaquero, or cowboy, rides after a longhorn steer. Steers like this sold for high prices during the Great Boom of the early 1850's.

Edward Borein

their boots, saddles trimmed with silver for their horses, silks and satins for their wives. They spent as much as two or three thousand dollars for a single outfit of fancy clothes.

When Congress passed the Land Act of 1851, the rancheros were puzzled. Under this law, they had to prove that their ranchos belonged to them. They shrugged their shoulders and went on enjoying themselves. Their families had been here for years. Everyone knew who owned the land. But proving it was not easy and cost money—much money. The rancheros began to borrow and soon they were in debt.

Meanwhile, ranchers from Texas, the Middle West, New Mexico, and Old Mexico, began bringing cattle to California. The price of steers dropped to fifty dollars, to thirty, to twenty-five, and less. By the late 1850's the Gold Rush was over, and so was the Great Boom in cattle.

From 1862 to 1864, nature itself seemed to turn against the rancheros. Drought dried up the springs and water-holes. The sun became an enemy, killing the grass and burning the earth to dust. Cattle died by the hundreds, by the thousands, and their skeletons lay in the fields. Clouds darkened the sky, but they brought no rain. They were clouds of locusts which settled on every growing thing for a terrible feast. Then an epidemic of smallpox struck down so many men, women, and children that the living cried out with fear whenever the church bell rang for the dead.

On the tax lists, cattle were valued at only a dollar a head, pasture land at ten cents an acre. The great ranchos were broken up. No more would the rancheros live like the Spanish dons, to the rumble of hoofs, the jingle of spurs, and the clang of guitars gleaming in the moonlight.

Years of change—change for the nation as well as for California. For, in 1861, the thunder of guns at Fort Sumter began the Civil War—the North against the South, the Union against the Confederacy. California stood by the Union. Sixteen thousand men enlisted in the Union Army, but the battlefields were far away, and few did any real fighting. California sent gold to the government in Washington, and raised more than a million dollars to help the sick and wounded. At the same time, there were many Californians who sided with the South, and some left to join the Confederates.

And when the war had ended, many things were different in the United States, just as they were in California. Years of change. . . .

Carl S. Dentzel Collection

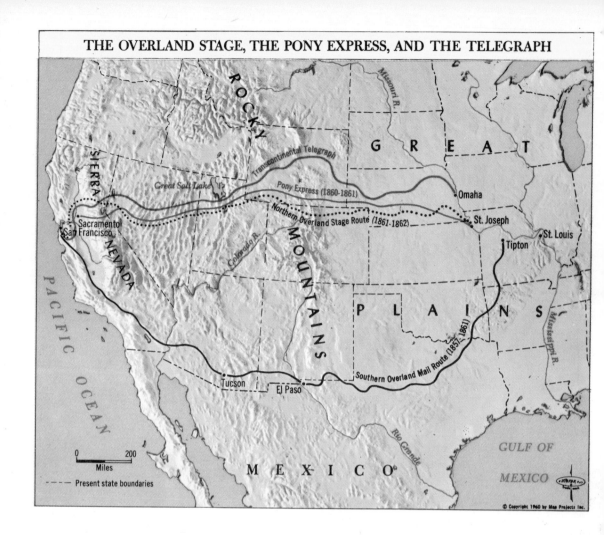

The Way to California

BUILDING THE RAILROAD TO THE PACIFIC

The first Spanish explorers believed that California was an island. And, separated from the rest of the world by mountains and the sea, it might as well have been an island. For years, reaching California meant a long, hard journey.

Even within California itself, travel was hard—and after the Gold Rush, people wanted to go places in a hurry. They were in just as much of a hurry to get goods and mail. The pack mules and *carretas* that had been used since the Spanish days were too slow. Freight and passengers could move faster by water,

and soon steamboats were sailing along the coast and up and down the rivers.

On land, freight was carried in big wagons. Passengers, gold, and mail were carried in stagecoaches. The stage driver, or "whip," as he called himself, was king of the road. With one hand, he held the reins of two or three pairs of horses. With the other hand, he cracked his whip, while he worked the brake with his foot. Winding down the mountains, racing along the valley trails, he drove at a speed of ten miles an hour. His passengers had a bouncing, jouncing, jolting, dusty ride, but, in spite of the discomfort, they got where they wanted to go.

Special stage lines ran between California and the end of the railroad in Missouri. The most famous of these lines was the Overland Mail. To set it up, John Butterfield and his partners spent a year of time and almost a million dollars in money. They bought 100 coaches, 1,500 horses, and 500 mules. They hired 150 drivers and 750 other workers. They built roads, bridges, ferries, and 165 stations. Laying out a route across the desert, they made sure their stages would not be stopped by winter snows. The line went from San Francisco to Los Angeles, then through the dangerous Indian country between Tucson and El Paso, and on to the end of the railroad at Tipton, Missouri.

On September 17, 1858, a stage started east from San Francisco while another started west from Tipton. A little after four o'clock on an October afternoon, the westbound stage clattered into San Francisco. It had traveled 2,800 miles in less than twenty-five days. Turn-

ing into Montgomery Street, the driver cracked his whip and blew his horn. People came rushing out, cheering and shouting. The driver raised his dusty, battered old hat and rode proudly through the crowds to the post office.

In 1860, a new kind of mail line—the Pony Express—was set up. It ran 1,966 miles from St. Joseph, Missouri, over the mountains to Sacramento. The Pony Express promised to deliver mail in no more than ten days. No stagecoaches would be used. Instead, daring riders would race across the wilderness on swift horses. They would ride for as much as seventy-five miles, changing horses at stations from ten to thirty miles apart.

Everything was planned for speed, and that meant the horses must carry as little weight as possible. Most of the riders were young—the average age was eighteen—and weighed no more than 145 pounds. They placed mail in pockets at the four corners of a *mochila*, a light leather covering which was slipped over the saddle. And the letters themselves had to be written on the thinnest paper.

Before the railroad, mountains cut off California from the other states.

Carl S. Dentzel Collection

Stagecoaches gave passengers a rough ride over dirt roads, but the only other ways of overland travel were on foot or on horseback.

On April 13, the first Pony Express rider to reach Sacramento came galloping up to the station on Second Street. Both horse and rider boarded a river boat to San Francisco. It was one o'clock in the morning when a great crowd of San Franciscans, carrying torches, met them at the wharf. To the music of brass bands they all paraded to the post office.

Just eighteen months later, the Pony Express made its last run. The swift little horses were sold, the riders looked for other jobs. Telegraph lines now stretched between San Francisco and the East, and on October 24, 1861, the first words went leaping along the wires:

The Pacific to the Atlantic sends greetings ; and may both oceans be dry before a foot of all the land that lies between shall belong to any other than one united country.

But the telegraph could carry only messages. Passengers, freight and much mail still traveled to California by stage, or by ship around Cape Horn, or by ship and mule over the land-sea route that crossed Panama. There were some improvements. Clipper ships, the fastest and most beautiful sailing vessels ever built, voyaged from New York to San Francisco, by way of Cape Horn, in as little as a hundred days. Steamboats hustled to and from Panama.

Even so, the way to California was long and hard, and the state still seemed like an island. Only a railroad could really unite the East and the West. And how could tracks be laid over the hundreds of miles of desert, and over the mountains that cut off California like a high stone wall?

Theodore D. Judah believed he knew how. A construction engineer, he had worked on canals and rail lines in the East. In 1854, he came to California to build the state's earliest railroad, twenty-two miles long, between Sacramento and Folsom.

After that, all Judah could think of was a Pacific railroad—a railroad that would go east over the Sierra Nevadas and across the continent. Searching for the best route, he made twenty-two trips to the mountains. Often he had to push through snowdrifts fifteen feet deep. He wrote reports about building a railroad and talked about it. Twice he visited Washington and talked to Congressmen about it. "Crazy Judah," people called him. He went on talking, until they began to listen.

At last, in a small room over a Sacramento hardware store, he talked to a group of businessmen. They agreed to put up money and form a company, the Central Pacific, to build the railroad. The most important officers of the company were Mark Hopkins and Collis P. Huntington, the owners of the hardware store; Leland Stanford, a wholesale grocer; and Charles Crocker, a dry-goods dealer. Later they became known as the Big Four.

Henry E. Huntington Library

Steamboats carried passengers along the coast.

Steamboats and sailing vessels made Sacramento a busy port.

Society of California Pioneers

Laying track along the side of a ridge helped to get the railroad over the Sierra Nevada Mountains. The Chinese workmen were called "Crocker's Pets," because they had been hired by Charles Crocker.

Again Judah went to Washington. He came back with the news that the government would give the company huge tracts of land and lend it large sums of money. Now the railroad would surely be built, and the happy Californians no longer called Judah crazy. But he and the Big Four quarreled. He thought their plans for making themselves fortunes were dishonest. He left California, hoping to raise enough money to buy the company. Crossing the Isthmus of Panama, he caught yellow fever. He died soon after he came ashore in New York, and the Big Four ruled the Central Pacific.

Work on the railroad had already begun, on January 8, 1863, at Sacramento. There was little trouble until the rails reached the mountains. Then gangs of workmen with picks, shovels, and wheelbarrows had to dig a roadway out of the steep sides of the Sierras. Tunnels had to be blasted through the rock. Snowsheds had to be built to keep the snow from piling up on the tracks. Food and supplies had to be hauled in on sleds.

The work was heavy, hard, and dangerous, and the men would not stay on the job. They ran off to Nevada, where silver had been found. Finally Crocker started hiring Chinese. Many Chinese lived in California, and he brought in more from China. By 1869 about 15,000 Chinese, still wearing their hair in long pigtails, were working on the railroad. "Crocker's Pets," as they were called, were small men and did not look very strong. But they brought the tracks over the mountains.

And after the mountains came the desert. For mile after mile it went on, with not a tree that could be cut down for ties. Wood—for ties, for shacks, even for the cooks' fires—had to be hauled to the men. Water, too, was scarce and had to be hauled in.

Meanwhile, the Irish workmen of another company, the Union Pacific, were laying track westward from Omaha. Somewhere the two rail lines would meet. For every mile of track, the Federal Government would give the builders thousands of acres of land and would lend thousands of dollars. Each company wanted as big a share as possible, and they raced to build the roadway—the Central Pacific against the Union Pacific, the Chinese workmen against the Irish, digging, blasting, pounding, driving across the continent.

In the spring of 1869 the two lines met at Promontory Point, Utah. On May 10, officers of the two companies, in top hats and long-tailed coats, made speeches and drove in a golden spike. Two locomotives touched cow-catchers. A band played. A message was sent by telegram to President Grant: *The last rail is laid, the last spike is driven. The Pacific Railroad is completed.*

No longer did California seem like an island.

Carl S. Dentzel Collection

1869. **May 10th.** 1869.
GREAT EVENT
Rail Road from the Atlantic to the Pacific
GRAND OPENING
— OF THE —
Union Pacific
RAIL ROAD,
PLATTE VALLEY ROUTE.
PASSENGER TRAINS LEAVE
OMAHA
ON THE ARRIVAL OF TRAINS FROM THE EAST.
THROUGH TO SAN FRANCISCO
In less than Four Days, avoiding the Dangers of the Sea!
Travelers for Pleasure, Health or Business
Will find a Trip over The Rocky Mountains Healthy and Pleasant.
LUXURIOUS CARS & EATING HOUSES
ON THE UNION PACIFIC RAIL ROAD.
PULLMAN'S PALACE SLEEPING CARS
RUN WITH ALL THROUGH PASSENGER TRAINS.
GOLD, SILVER AND OTHER MINERS!
Now is the time to seek your Fortunes in Nebraska, Wyoming, Arizona, Washington, Dakotah Colorado, Utah, Oregon, Montana, New Mexico, Idaho, Nevada or California.
CONNECTIONS MADE AT
CHEYENNE for DENVER, CENTRAL CITY & SANTA FE
AT OGDEN AND CORINNE FOR HELENA, BOISE CITY, VIRGINIA CITY, SALT LAKE CITY AND ARIZONA.
THROUGH TICKETS FOR SALE AT ALL PRINCIPAL RAILROAD OFFICES!
Be Sure they Read via Platte Valley or Omaha
Company's Office 72 La Salle St., opposite City Hall and Court House Square, Chicago.
CHARLES E. NICHOLS, Ticket Agent.
G. P. GILMAN.   JOHN P. HART.   J. BUDD.   W. SNYDER.

Union Pacific Railroad

Heavy snows in the mountains often blocked the tracks of the Central Pacific Railroad, stopping supply trains. Then wooden sheds (left) were built over the tracks. Altogether, forty miles of such snowsheds were constructed. At last, after years of work, posters like the one above announced the opening of the railroad. California was linked to the Eastern states.

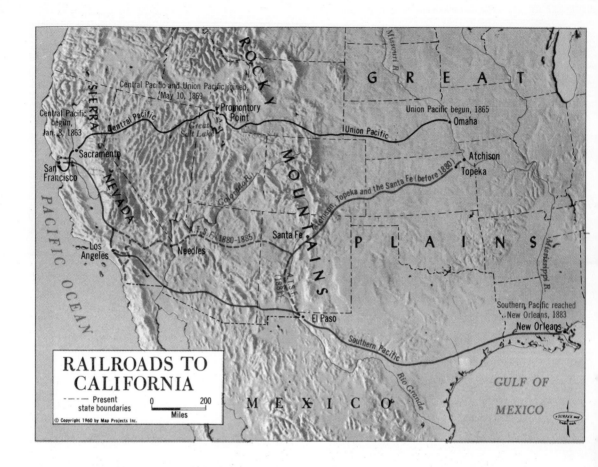

RAILROADS TO CALIFORNIA
- - - - Present state boundaries
0 200 Miles
© Copyright 1960 by Map Projects Inc.

The Sound of Locomotives

THE RAILROAD BRINGS PEOPLE AND A LAND BOOM

Rolling along the Central Pacific's shining rails, trains crossed the mountains to California. The Big Four had piled up fortunes for themselves, but they had built a railroad. They went on building railroads, shorter lines that linked towns inside the state. The puff and chug of locomotives, the wailing whistles and rumbling wheels, made a new sound in the land.

There were other new sounds as well—the bleating of enormous flocks of sheep, the clank of machinery threshing wheat, the creak of rigs drilling for oil.

After the rains ended the great drought, sheep by the thousands munched on the green grass. Sheep had been raised in California before, but never had there been so many. By 1873, they numbered nearly 4,000,000.

In the great Central Valley, wheat grew for mile after mile, turning yellow in the hot sun. The wheat ranches were huge, some of them covering 50,000 acres. At harvest time, golden clouds of dust rose while gangs of men worked with threshing machines to gather in the grain. By 1889, California was growing more wheat than any other state in the Union except Minnesota.

And here and there, in scattered places, men brought oil up from the earth.

With the new sounds, many of the old sounds were still heard. Cattle bawled in the

San Joaquin and Sacramento valleys. They were raised, not by rancheros, but by cattlemen who owned even larger herds and tracts of land. Henry Miller and Charles Lux started a cattle business that in time had 1,000,000 head of livestock and more than 1,000,000 acres of grazing land in California, Nevada, and Oregon.

From much smaller tracts of land came the voices of men tending farms and orchards and vineyards. Just as they had since mission days, Californians grew grapes and made wine— 2,000,000 gallons of it by 1870. Oranges, too, had first been grown at the missions. For years the only really large groves were at Los Angeles, where William Wolfskill had set out his trees in 1841. Thirty-two years later, Mrs. Eliza Tibbetts planted two trees brought over from Brazil. They bore seedless navel oranges, the finest ever seen in America. Other growers planted shoots from these same trees, and oranges became California's leading crop.

The small farmers did not have any easy time. They had to learn the right way to work the land. They had to fight off grasshoppers, gophers, squirrels, coyotes—and jackrabbits. Often the farmers held "rabbit drives." While a band played lively music, a line of several hundred men, on foot and on horseback, would march across the fields. They drove the rabbits into a corral made of wire fence and clubbed them to death.

The sound of locomotives first came to southern California with the building of small, local railroads. In 1876, a rail line was completed between Los Angeles and San Francisco. The Big Four had offered to bring their new line, the Southern Pacific, to the town—if Los Angeles gave them a loan of $600,000, sixty acres of land for a station, and control of a small railroad that was already built. The Angelenos finally agreed, and in 1876 the first train rolled in.

By 1887, the tracks of the Atchison, Topeka and Santa Fe railroad reached Los Angeles. The Big Four owned no part of this line and

William Wolfskill's orange groves in Los Angeles covered 100 acres by 1861.

California's first oil refinery was set up in 1875.

fought it by lowering fares. The Santa Fe fought back. On the walls of ticket offices, signs went up:

WHOOPLA! First-class to Kansas City, Deming and El Paso, $15; third-class, $10; Chicago and St. Louis, $17 and $15; New York, $30 and $27.

Down she goes. Lower! Lower!! Lowest!!! Kansas City, $12 and $10; Chicago and St. Louis, $17 and $15; New York, $30 and $27.

Fares were lowered again and again. For a while, tickets for the trip between Los Angeles and Kansas City were selling for three dollars, two dollars, one dollar. The chug of locomotives driving westward seemed to echo over all America. The whistles seemed to sing a song of sunlit skies and green valleys, of shining mountains, ocean beaches and sweet-smelling orange groves.

Californians formed "booster" organizations to tell the world about their state. In books and newspapers, in pamphlets and handbills, they invited people to California. The railroads had land to sell, and their agents also spread the word. Come to California! Come for health! Come for wealth! Come to see! Come to stay! Golden California, where spring lasts forever! No frost, no snow, no slush! Come to California!

Down went the fares, and in came the people, especially to southern California. They hoped to buy and sell land, or to raise oranges, or to farm. All of them hoped for an easier life in the sun. Those with enough money traveled in fairly comfortable first-class cars. Those with less money traveled in special emigrant cars, where they sat, slept, and did their own cooking.

In came the people—and up went the price of land. Towns were laid out on swamps, on deserts, on hillsides. Before they had even left

During the 1880's, tons of borax, a mineral used in industry, were dug up in Death Valley. "Twenty-mule teams" (above) hauled wagons full of borax 165 miles to the railroad at Mojave. The round trip took about twenty days.

Low railroad fares brought people flocking to Southern California, anxious to buy land. Real estate men, sometimes using tents for offices (below), attracted crowds with free rides, free lunches, bands, and even elephants.

Horse cars still rolled on Spring Street, Los Angeles, in 1885.

the railroad station at Los Angeles, new-comers were given handbills:

PURE GOLD! PURE GOLD!
Come Get It!
The Metropolis of Southern California's
Fairest Valley!

QUEEN OF THEM ALL
lovely

LOVELY

L O V E L Y

Beautiful! Busy! Bustling! Bountiful! Booming!

CAN'T BEAT IT!
It's a big, big, BOOM! It's a big, big, BOOM!

A GREAT BIG BOOM!
And you?

CAN ACCUMULATE DUCATS BY INVESTING!

COME TO GLORIOUS SANTA ANA

(free lunch)   *(free music)*

SEE IT! SEE IT! SEE IT!

Carriages and wagons waited to take them to the new towns—free. At the end of the ride, lunch was dished out—free. Bands played. Fast-talking salesmen moved among the crowds, shouting:

"Here she is! Look 'er over!"

Not that there was much to see. The raw land lay under the bright sky, the lots marked off with white stakes. There might be a few signposts with the names of streets, or a big wooden building not quite finished.

"That's the hotel, folks. Just going up! She'll be the busiest town in California. Buy your lots now! Buy today, before it's too late! They'll be worth double in a week! Buy now!"

And the people bought. They bought and sold, bought and sold, while prices kept going up. It was a boom, a boom, a great big boom, and no mistake.

Suddenly, in 1888, the price of land fell. The big boom was over. Packed trains left Los Angeles, carrying people east, carrying them home. And yet, many stayed. From 1880 to 1887, the population of Los Angeles had grown from 11,183 to more than 70,000. After the boom, it still had 50,395 persons. The state itself had grown from 865,000 in 1880 to 1,200,000 in 1890.

The new settlers were Americans, mainly from the Midwest. They had no memory of old California. They cared little for the reminders of the Spanish or Mexican days.

They cared just as little for the Indians. The California Indians were poor creatures anyway, and they were dying out. For some time the government had been moving them to reservations. The Indians fought against it in little "wars," like the Modoc War of 1873. That year, several hundred Modoc Indians, from the northern part of the state, ran off to the lava beds near Tule Lake. It cost half a million dollars and the lives of almost a hundred Americans to round them up. But that was the last of the Indian wars.

No one could doubt that California belonged to Americans. After the Central Pacific railroad was built, work was hard to find. Californians were afraid that the Chinese would take their jobs for less pay. In San Francisco, workmen paraded the streets, shouting "The Chinese must go!" In more than one town, Chinese homes and laundries were burned. A mob of Angelenos raided the Chinese section and hanged twenty-two Chinese. When a new state constitution was voted in 1879, it contained laws that made it more difficult for the Chinese to stay in California. And, in 1882, Congress passed a law keeping Chinese out of the United States.

Yes, Californians were Americans—and times were hard for Americans in the 1890's. Thousands of men who had lost their jobs drifted in from other states. Breadlines were set up.

Californians shook their heads and wondered what was happening to the country. But the sun—the glorious, golden sun—still shone, the air was soft, the valleys were green. Tomorrow the sun would shine again, and, sooner or later, things would get better.

A number of ways of transportation are shown in this scene of San Diego.

Society of California Pioneers

San Francisco City Hall in ruins after the earthquake and fire

A Tale of Two Cities

SAN FRANCISCO AND LOS ANGELES TALK BUSINESS

It was the night of April 17, 1906. In San Francisco, clanging red-and-yellow cable cars rode the steep hills, carrying people home from the theaters. Carriages pulled up before the crowd leaving the Grand Opera House. Some of the carriages rolled off to the huge mansions of the rich on Nob Hill. Others clattered over the cobblestones to the brightly lighted restaurants, noisy with laughter and the clink of wineglasses.

Still brightly lighted, too, were the restaurants of Chinatown, the section where the Chinese lived. Chattering in their strange tongue, the sons and grandsons of the men who had built the railroad scooped up rice with chopsticks. Near Pacific Avenue and Kearny Street, sailors of a dozen nations thronged the dance-halls and drinking places.

They had sailed through the Golden Gate, the narrow entrance to the great harbor, and now their ships were tied up at the dark wharves.

San Francisco was far different from the first little Spanish settlement on the bay. Yerba Buena, it was called then—the Good Herb—because of the thick grass on the sand dunes. The name was changed in 1847, a year before gold was discovered. By 1906 San Francisco was the largest city on the west coast, with tall office buildings, fine homes, schools, libraries, and newspapers. The population was about 400,000, and it was still growing.

Perhaps it was growing too fast. At least, the members of the Press Club were beginning to think so. A tall building had been put up beside their clubhouse, cutting off air and light. Soon a second tall building would rise on the other side. That April night, the members held a special meeting, discussing whether or not the club should move.

After the meeting, Wilbur G. Zeigler stayed to chat with a few friends. The talk was pleasant, the room was comfortable, and the hours went quickly. When he left the club, he was surprised to see the soft gray light of dawn. He glanced at his watch. It was a little past five o'clock, on the morning of April 18.

He bought a newspaper from a newsboy and, turning into Powell Street, stopped at a corner store for some cigars. He leaned over to get a light from a small lamp that hung from a cord. For no reason at all, the lamp swung away from him. He made a grab for the cord, but the floor shook under his feet, and he missed. The next moment he felt himself thrown against the counter, while from the restaurant in the basement below came a tremendous crash of glass.

The storekeeper, his face white, leaped over the counter. Zeigler ran outside with the storekeeper following. Four men were rushing up the stairs from the basement restaurant. One of them sobbed as they knelt on the sidewalk and prayed.

Suddenly a grinding roar rose from the city. Zeigler stared at the Columbia Theater, on the other side of the street. The upper part of the building bulged, sagged, and tumbled to the pavement. Looking around in amazement, Zeigler saw the Flood Building sway out and back again like a live thing. He knew what was happening. This was an earthquake, the worst in the history of California.

Everywhere in the city, people were looking around in amazement, just as Zeigler was doing. Sidewalks buckled and broke. Huge cracks opened up in the earth. The walls of buildings shifted and split. Pillars toppled. Houses twisted and roofs slid. Brick, stone, wood, plaster crumbled and piled up in heaps.

The earthquake lasted less than four minutes —and then came fire. No fog rolled in from the sea to dampen the flames; no rain fell. Beyond the haze of black smoke, the sky was bright and clear. Fire engines sped through the streets. But the quakes had broken the water mains, and the hoses were dry.

Thousands of San Franciscans lost their homes in the great fire.

This photograph, taken after the earthquake and fire of 1906, shows San Francisco in ruins. But repairing and rebuilding had already started, and a new city quickly rose from the ashes and wreckage.

For three days and two nights the fire burned. Twenty-eight thousand buildings, covering four square miles, were destroyed. The entire business district was in ruins. At least five hundred persons were killed. Thousands of others were homeless. They crowded into tents put up in the parks and on the beaches. Some left the city, carrying bundles of whatever belongings they had been able to save. Luckier ones drove wagons loaded with trunks and furniture. Soldiers guarded the streets, with orders to shoot anyone caught stealing.

Even before the fire had died down, while hot smoke billowed and cinders flew through the air, San Franciscans began to smile. On a tent in Jefferson Park was this sign: WELL SHOOK. The sign on the next tent said: SHOOK WELL. On a pile of bricks—almost all that remained of a business building—someone propped a sign: WE MOVED BE-

CAUSE THE ELEVATOR WASN'T RUNNING. A piano, hauled away from a burning home on a wagon, carried a sign that read: PLAYED ON BY MANY—LAST TIME BY A FIREMAN.

The Mayor set up a Committee of Fifty to run the city. Money, food, clothing, medicine, tools poured in from the rest of the nation. Signs were put up in the streets: DON'T TALK EARTHQUAKE, TALK BUSINESS. The wreckage was cleared, and San Francisco began to rebuild. In less than three years, the job was done.

But, for a long time, newcomers to the state were afraid to settle in San Francisco. Instead, they flocked to southern California, especially to Los Angeles. The city grew from a population of about 100,000 in 1900 to 319,000 in 1910. It spread until it covered 451 square miles. Angelenos were not satisfied with

land; they wanted a way to the sea. In 1899 they began building an artificial harbor at San Pedro, and over the years they developed a large port.

Oil, automobiles, motion pictures, farms, land, sunshine—all of these helped southern California and Los Angeles grow. In 1893, E. L. Doheny and C. A. Canfield struck oil in the front yard of a home at Patton and West State Streets. Soon 1,400 derricks rose in the city. Other oil fields were discovered in southern California, and the state was producing 77,000,000 barrels of oil by 1910, 104,000,000 by 1914.

It was the automobile that made oil valuable, and automobiles brought still more people to California. The state's first paved road for cars was built in 1912. The speed limit was six miles an hour in business districts, eight miles an hour in residential districts. During the early 1900's, thousands of dollars were spent to build good roads. Along the King's Highway, where the Spanish had once traveled by horse and mule, rolled cars, trucks and buses.

Meanwhile, in a quiet section of Los Angeles called Hollywood, a new kind of industry was beginning. In October of 1911 the Horsley Brothers bought a tavern and barn at Sunset Boulevard and Gower Street. Here they made a motion picture, *The Law of the Range.* Within a few years, other movie makers had followed them to Hollywood. Actors dressed as kings and clowns and cowboys strolled the streets. Hollywood and its movie stars became known all over the world.

At the same time, farmers still worked the land of southern California. Down irrigation canals and ditches flowed water for the dry desert regions. Oranges, lemons, walnuts, grapes, raisins, prunes, figs, cotton were picked and packed and prepared and shipped by train to the East and Midwest.

Making a movie in the early days of silent pictures

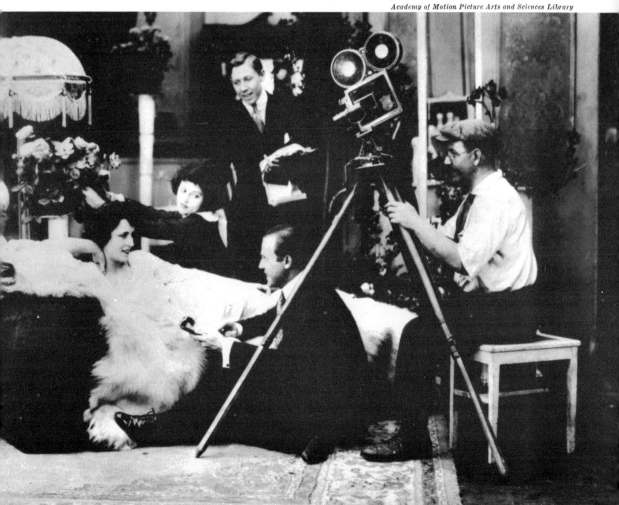

Vast orange groves helped make California first in farming of all the states.

And from the East and Midwest, by train and car, came people—old couples who wanted a mild climate, youngsters who wanted to see the movie stars, men who wanted to work in the fields or get rich or just live a good life in the sun. They had read advertisements of a climate "to suit everyone . . . no winter and no summer in Los Angeles . . . no depressing heat, no insect pests . . . a climate that makes the sick well and the strong more vigorous."

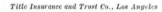

Once again, in 1921, there was a land boom. Again bands played, and free lunches were served. Again fast-talking salesmen moved among the crowds, shouting, "Buy now, folks! Tomorrow may be too late! Sign up for your land today! Sign on the dotted line! Live and get rich in happy, healthy California!"

New oil fields were discovered at Huntington Beach, Long Beach, and Santa Fe Springs, and there was an oil boom as well as a land boom. Factories of all kinds sprang up, and by 1925 Los Angeles was one of the nation's leading manufacturing cities. The harbor was busy with ships carrying oil, lumber, and cotton. The invention of sound pictures made the movie industry mightier than ever.

In the rest of the country, too, business was booming. Herbert Hoover, the first Californian to be elected President, moved into the White House. His party promised a chicken in every pot and a car in every garage. But by 1929 the boom was over—not only in Los Angeles, not only in California, but everywhere in the United States.

Oil pours from a "gusher" at Long Beach.

Los Angeles in 1848 was far different from the great city it is today.

The Golden Land

CALIFORNIA CONTINUES TO GROW

In the early years of the 1930's, tourists driving to southern California wondered what was happening. More and more often, they had to swing over and pass some rattling jalopy making its slow way west on the long road. Crowded into the jalopy would be a whole family. All of the family's belongings seemed to be packed in the car or tied to the top and sides—a washtub, blankets, mattresses, a rocking chair, a broom, a mop, boxes of dishes and pots and pans.

The tourists stared at the worried man behind the wheel, at the old couple beside him, at the thin-faced children jammed with the mother in the back seat. Who were these people? Where did they come from? Where were they going?

The people in the jalopies had been farmers in the states of the western plains. Then a terrible drought dried and crumbled the earth, turning it into a huge Dust Bowl. Winds blew up dust storms that hid the sun. The corn drooped and sickened. Cattle starved and died. At even the slightest breeze, dust rose in the air, stinging the eyes and tasting bitter on the tongue.

The farmers were forced to leave and find work. But where could they go? For it was hard times, hard times, in the U.S.A. A great depression, the worst in the nation's history, was closing factories and shops. Everywhere in the countryside farmers were losing their farms; in the cities men were begging for jobs.

But word spread across the Dust Bowl that there was work in California. California needed men to pick its fruit and vegetables. California ... the golden land, the land of plenty, the land of sunshine and movie stars and crops that seemed to grow overnight.

Scraping together a few dollars for a jalopy, the farmers piled in everything they owned and started west. "Okies," they were called,

Their farms ruined by drought, Okies looked for work in California.

because so many of them came from Oklahoma. They did find work in California—but only during the six or seven months of the harvest season. The pay was low and dropped even lower as more Okies came in. And, after the harvest, they were not welcomed.

"When they need us," an Okie once said, "they call us migrants. When we've picked their crop, we're bums and we got to get out."

It was not the first time that Californians feared and mistrusted newcomers. They had passed laws against the Chinese, shouting, "The Chinese must go!" Later they said the same thing about the Japanese, and they were troubled by the Filipinos and the thousands of Mexicans who came to work in the fields. The Japanese were skillful gardeners and farmers, and in 1913 the Alien Land Act was passed to keep them from owning land.

In spite of the laws, the Chinese and the Japanese remained. The "Chinatowns" in San Francisco and Los Angeles became famous. By 1920 there were 72,000 Japanese in California, and the Japanese district in Los Angeles

was known as "Little Tokyo." At least 250,000 Mexicans were living in California by 1930, and Los Angeles had more Mexicans than any city in the world except Mexico City.

No laws could be passed to keep out the Okies. They were citizens whose families had lived in America for many years. They kept coming to California—perhaps 350,000 of them between 1930 and 1940—for it was hard times, hard times, and a man had to find some way to keep his family alive.

The farms and orchards they worked on were huge, many covering a thousand acres or more. They were run more like factories than farms, and were often called "factories in the fields." Like factory workers, the Okies and other workers in the fields sometimes went on strike for higher pay, fewer hours, and better working conditions. In the cities, too, men were joining unions and going on strike. A hundred thousand persons went on strike in San Francisco's great general strike in 1934. Two strikers were killed in battles with police, and 10,000 union men marched in their funeral.

Hard times, and when they would end no one could say. Many organizations were formed with all sorts of ideas to end the depression. Old people formed organizations to work for pensions. Hard times . . . and still California grew. The population rose from 5,677,251 in 1930 to 6,907,387 in 1940.

To meet the needs of the growing cities, aqueducts were built to bring water to Los Angeles and San Francisco. The Federal Government built Hoover Dam in Nevada. In 1935 the gates of the dam were closed, storing water from the Colorado River to irrigate the dry lands of California. And in 1937 San Francisco opened its Golden Gate Bridge. The main span, the longest in the world, crossed the bay in a giant leap of 4,200 feet.

Then, in 1941, Japan bombed Pearl Harbor. The United States was at war with Japan and Germany, and needed men to fight and make the weapons of war. Thousands of Californians joined the armed forces. Other thousands went to work in the factories and fields. Still other thousands of men and women came flocking to the state to work beside them.

Huge airplane factories went up at Burbank, Santa Monica, El Segundo, Inglewood, Long Beach, San Diego. Along the coast, shipyards turned out vessel after vessel. Steel mills were set up, and shops to make parts for airplanes and ships. From the oil wells came millions of barrels of oil, and from the farms and ranches came food by the ton. Huge army and navy camps and bases trained men from every state in the Union.

The shriek of sirens in air-raid tests reminded Californians that they could be attacked by Japan. And if they were, could they trust the 127,000 Japanese who now lived in California? True, about 80,000 of these Japanese were American citizens. Many were Nisei, or American-born.

Even so, a number of Californians were suspicious. Soon the Federal Government moved thousands of Japanese from the Pacific Coast to camps were they were kept under guard. At the same time, Nisei soldiers drafted into the army fought bravely for the United States.

Union Pacific Railroad

Since its earliest days, visitors and tourists have come to see the wonders of California. Among the sights are the giant trees in Sequoia National Park (above), and Chinatown and the cable cars in San Francisco (below).

Union Pacific Railroad

Walt Disney's Disneyland has become famous throughout the world.

In 1945 a conference to set up the United Nations was held in San Francisco. The war was over, and few people believed that California would continue to grow. Surely the workers in the war plants would go back to their home states. Instead, they stayed. Soldiers who had been stationed in California returned with their families. Tourists who had only heard of California came to see it for themselves—and they, too, stayed.

California grew faster than ever. By 1950, the population was 10,586,223; by 1955, more than 12,000,000; by 1960 about 15,537,413. Newcomers were pouring in—almost 1,500 a day, 50,000 a year. They came by car, by bus, by train, by plane, by swift jets that could cross the continent in five and a half hours. They came for the climate, for jobs, for a different kind of living.

Because California was still a golden land of plenty. Among the states, it was second in population, third in area. It was first in farming, second in oil production, and the Los Angeles district was the third largest center of

Cars travel at high speed over Los Angeles' system of freeways.

Union Pacific Railroad

The largest vessels can easily pass under San Francisco's Golden Gate Bridge (above), longest single-span suspension bridge in the world.

California busily prepares for the future with its rocket, aviation, and electronic industries. Below is shown a rocket-machine testing station.

Rocketdyne, a Division of North American Aviation, Inc.

manufacturing. It was first in cars and swimming pools. It had the largest bank, the largest missile base, the largest aircraft and rocket and electronics factories. It had famous universities, libraries, and centers of scientific research.

It had problems, too. Around Los Angeles, San Francisco, and San Diego spread acre after acre of new houses. Old-time Californians complained that the state was getting too crowded. In spite of miles of new highways, the roads were clogged with traffic. Smog often dirtied the air above Los Angeles.

And still the people came. Like the Forty-Niners, like the pioneers who had pushed across deserts and mountains, they had great hopes for the future. In their own way, they were singing:

> *Oh, California!*
> *That's the land for me!*
> *I'm bound for Californy*
> *With my washbowl on my knee!*

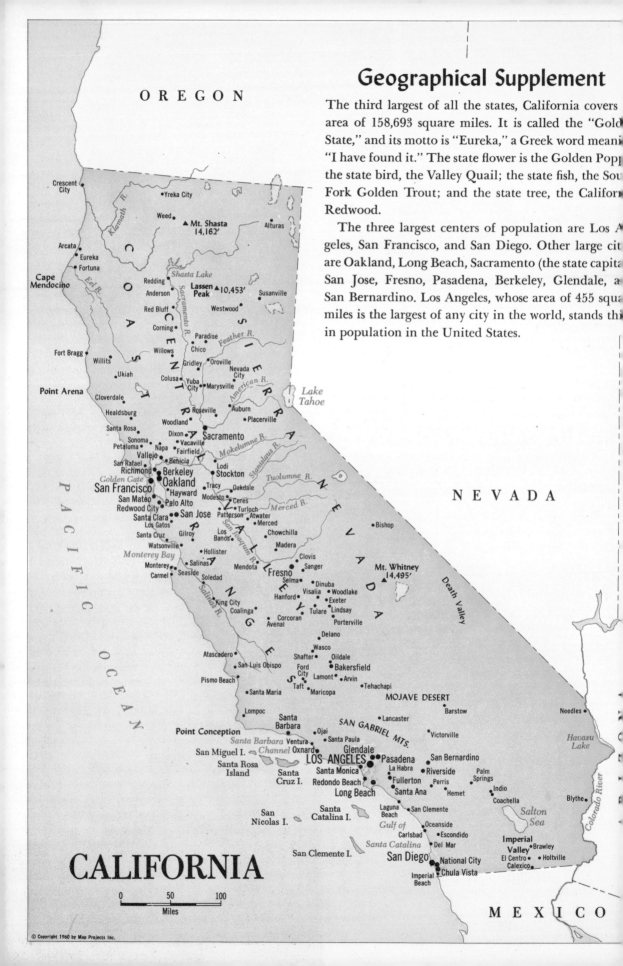

Geographical Supplement

The third largest of all the states, California covers [an] area of 158,693 square miles. It is called the "Gold[en] State," and its motto is "Eureka," a Greek word mean[ing] "I have found it." The state flower is the Golden Popp[y]; the state bird, the Valley Quail; the state fish, the Sou[th] Fork Golden Trout; and the state tree, the Califor[nia] Redwood.

The three largest centers of population are Los A[n]geles, San Francisco, and San Diego. Other large cit[ies] are Oakland, Long Beach, Sacramento (the state capita[l]), San Jose, Fresno, Pasadena, Berkeley, Glendale, a[nd] San Bernardino. Los Angeles, whose area of 455 squa[re] miles is the largest of any city in the world, stands thi[rd] in population in the United States.

CALIFORNIA

0   50   100
Miles

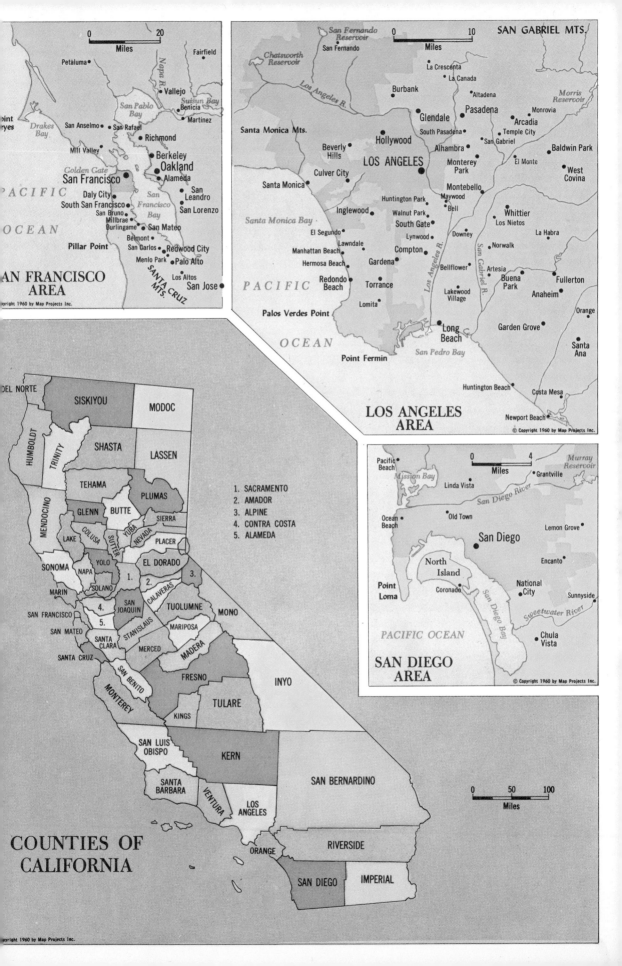

SAN FRANCISCO AREA

Fairfield
Petaluma
Napa R.
Point Reyes
Drakes Bay
San Pablo Bay
Vallejo
Suisun Bay
Benicia
Martinez
San Anselmo
San Rafael
Richmond
Mill Valley
Berkeley
Oakland
San Francisco
Golden Gate
Alameda
PACIFIC
San Francisco Bay
Daly City
San Leandro
South San Francisco
San Lorenzo
San Bruno
Millbrae
Burlingame
San Mateo
OCEAN
Belmont
San Carlos
Redwood City
Pillar Point
Menlo Park
Palo Alto
Los Altos
San Jose
SANTA CRUZ MTS.
Copyright 1960 by Map Projects Inc.

Miles 0 20

LOS ANGELES AREA

SAN GABRIEL MTS.
Miles 0 10
San Fernando Reservoir
Chatsworth Reservoir
San Fernando
La Crescenta
La Canada
Los Angeles R.
Burbank
Altadena
Morris Reservoir
Glendale
Pasadena
Monrovia
Arcadia
Santa Monica Mts.
Hollywood
South Pasadena
Temple City
Beverly Hills
Alhambra
San Gabriel
Baldwin Park
LOS ANGELES
Monterey Park
El Monte
West Covina
Culver City
Santa Monica
Montebello
Whittier
Huntington Park
Maywood
Los Nietos
Inglewood
Walnut Park
Bell
La Habra
Santa Monica Bay
South Gate
El Segundo
Lynwood
Downey
Norwalk
Manhattan Beach
Lawndale
Compton
Bellflower
Artesia
Buena Park
Hermosa Beach
Gardena
Fullerton
Redondo Beach
Torrance
Lakewood Village
Anaheim
PACIFIC
Lomita
Orange
Palos Verdes Point
San Gabriel R.
Los Angeles R.
Garden Grove
OCEAN
Long Beach
Santa Ana
Point Fermin
San Pedro Bay
Huntington Beach
Costa Mesa
Newport Beach
© Copyright 1960 by Map Projects Inc.

SAN DIEGO AREA

Miles 0 4
Pacific Beach
Murray Reservoir
Mission Bay
Linda Vista
Grantville
San Diego River
Ocean Beach
Old Town
Lemon Grove
San Diego
Encanto
North Island
National City
Sunnyside
Point Loma
Coronado
San Diego Bay
Sweetwater River
PACIFIC OCEAN
Chula Vista
© Copyright 1960 by Map Projects Inc.

COUNTIES OF CALIFORNIA

DEL NORTE
SISKIYOU
MODOC
HUMBOLDT
TRINITY
SHASTA
LASSEN
TEHAMA
MENDOCINO
GLENN
BUTTE
PLUMAS
SIERRA
COLUSA
LAKE
YUBA
NEVADA
SUTTER
PLACER
YOLO
EL DORADO
SONOMA
NAPA
1.
3.
MARIN
SOLANO
2.
CALAVERAS
TUOLUMNE
MONO
SAN FRANCISCO
4.
SAN JOAQUIN
5.
STANISLAUS
MARIPOSA
SAN MATEO
SANTA CLARA
MERCED
MADERA
SANTA CRUZ
FRESNO
INYO
SAN BENITO
MONTEREY
TULARE
KINGS
SAN LUIS OBISPO
KERN
SAN BERNARDINO
SANTA BARBARA
VENTURA
LOS ANGELES
ORANGE
RIVERSIDE
SAN DIEGO
IMPERIAL

1. SACRAMENTO
2. AMADOR
3. ALPINE
4. CONTRA COSTA
5. ALAMEDA

Miles 0 50 100

Copyright 1960 by Map Projects Inc.

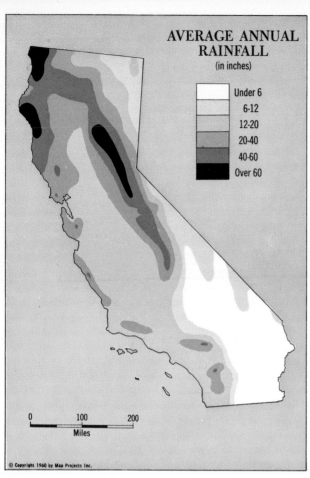

AVERAGE ANNUAL RAINFALL
(in inches)

	Under 6
	6-12
	12-20
	20-40
	40-60
	Over 60

0   100   200
Miles

© Copyright 1960 by Map Projects Inc.

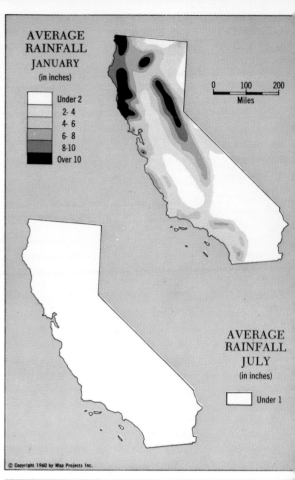

AVERAGE RAINFALL JANUARY
(in inches)

	Under 2
	2-4
	4-6
	6-8
	8-10
	Over 10

0   100   200
Miles

AVERAGE RAINFALL JULY
(in inches)

	Under 1

© Copyright 1960 by Map Projects Inc.

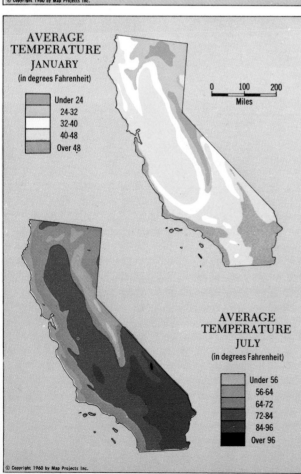

AVERAGE TEMPERATURE JANUARY
(in degrees Fahrenheit)

	Under 24
	24-32
	32-40
	40-48
	Over 48

0   100   200
Miles

AVERAGE TEMPERATURE JULY
(in degrees Fahrenheit)

	Under 56
	56-64
	64-72
	72-84
	84-96
	Over 96

© Copyright 1960 by Map Projects Inc.

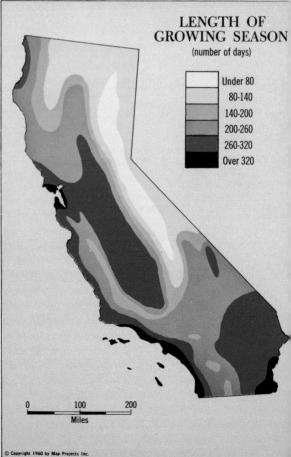

LENGTH OF GROWING SEASON
(number of days)

	Under 80
	80-140
	140-200
	200-260
	260-320
	Over 320

0   100   200
Miles

© Copyright 1960 by Map Projects Inc.

Recreation

Within the borders of California are four national parks, eighteen national forests, eight national monuments, and more than 150 state parks. Along the coast are many miles of beaches, and inland there are about 8,000 lakes with a surface area of at least five acres.

In Inyo National Park is a stand of bristlecone pine believed to be 4,500 years old, making it the oldest living thing on earth. The General Sherman tree, a giant sequoia in Sequoia National Park, is 272.4 feet high, 36.5 feet in diameter, and is believed to be between 3,000 and 4,000 years old.

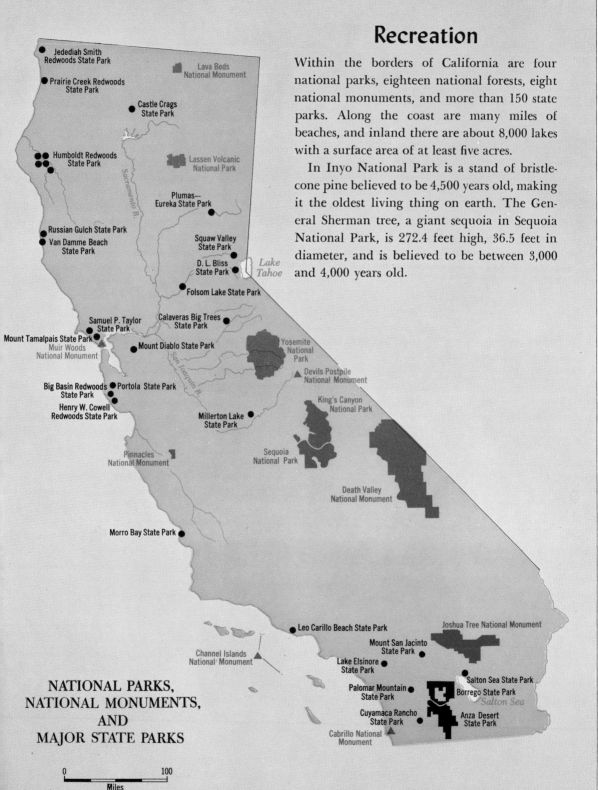

Jedediah Smith
Redwoods State Park

Lava Beds
National Monument

Prairie Creek Redwoods
State Park

Castle Crags
State Park

Humboldt Redwoods
State Park

Lassen Volcanic
National Park

Plumas—
Eureka State Park

Russian Gulch State Park

Van Damme Beach
State Park

Squaw Valley
State Park

D. L. Bliss
State Park

Lake Tahoe

Folsom Lake State Park

Samuel P. Taylor
State Park

Calaveras Big Trees
State Park

Mount Tamalpais State Park

Muir Woods
National Monument

Mount Diablo State Park

Yosemite
National
Park

Devils Postpile
National Monument

Big Basin Redwoods
State Park

Portola State Park

King's Canyon
National Park

Henry W. Cowell
Redwoods State Park

Millerton Lake
State Park

Pinnacles
National Monument

Sequoia
National Park

Death Valley
National Monument

Morro Bay State Park

Leo Carillo Beach State Park

Joshua Tree National Monument

Mount San Jacinto
State Park

Channel Islands
National Monument

Lake Elsinore
State Park

Salton Sea State Park

Palomar Mountain
State Park

Borrego State Park

Salton Sea

Cuyamaca Rancho
State Park

Anza Desert
State Park

Cabrillo National
Monument

Sacramento R.

San Joaquin R.

NATIONAL PARKS,
NATIONAL MONUMENTS,
AND
MAJOR STATE PARKS

0   100
Miles

Agriculture, Minerals, and Industry

California leads all the states in the production of fruit, vegetables, and wine. Among the crops are oranges, lemons, peaches, grapes, pears, apricots, plums, prunes, cherries, avocados; almonds, walnuts, olives, figs, barley, beans, beets, lettuce, and cotton. On the grazing lands, cattle and sheep are raised.

California ranks second in the production of crude oil, third in gold. More than sixty minerals are produced, including cement, borax, iron, tungsten, copper, and silver.

The state is first in fishing and second in lumbering. Food processing is the leading industry, followed by the manufacturing of transportation equipment, including aircraft, ships, and automobiles. Electronics is a rapidly growing industry.

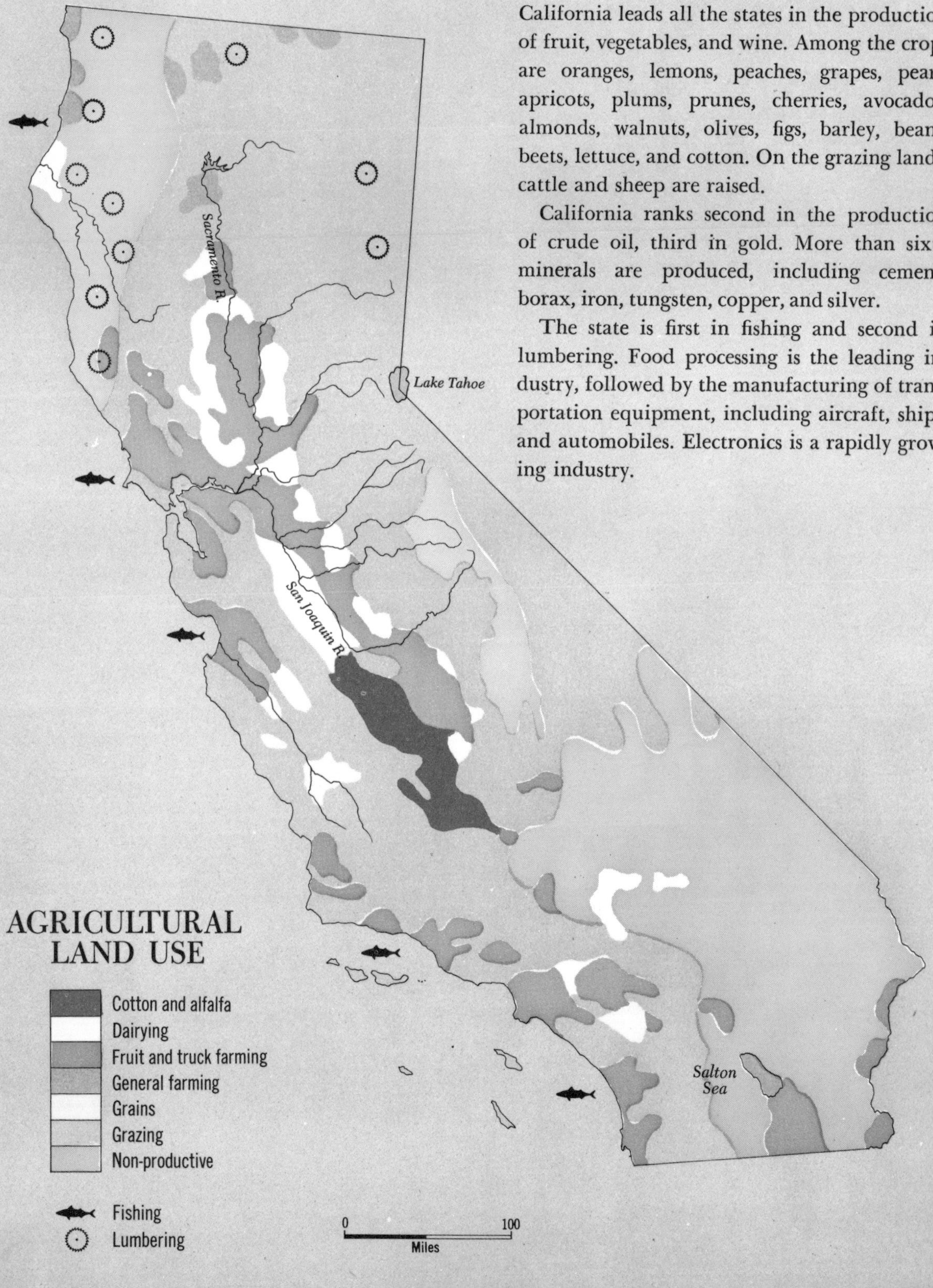

Sacramento R.

Lake Tahoe

San Joaquin R.

Salton Sea

AGRICULTURAL LAND USE

- Cotton and alfalfa
- Dairying
- Fruit and truck farming
- General farming
- Grains
- Grazing
- Non-productive

Fishing

Lumbering

0   100
Miles

after Focus – A.G

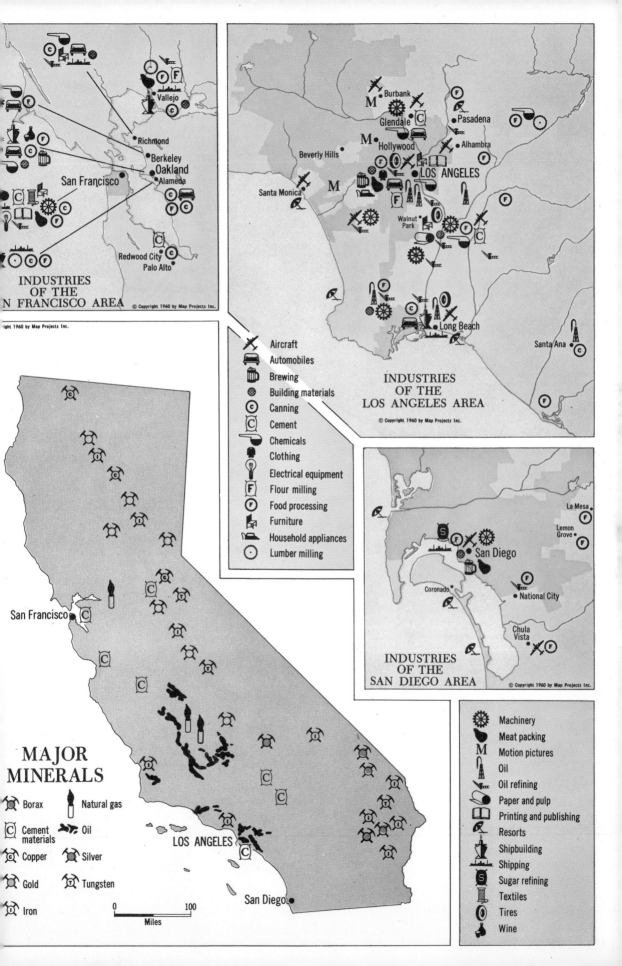

INDUSTRIES
OF THE
SAN FRANCISCO AREA

© Copyright 1960 by Map Projects Inc.

Vallejo

Richmond

Berkeley
Oakland
Alameda

San Francisco

Redwood City
Palo Alto

© Copyright 1960 by Map Projects Inc.

Burbank

Glendale
Beverly Hills
Hollywood
Santa Monica
Alhambra

LOS ANGELES
Pasadena

Walnut
Park

Long Beach

Santa Ana

INDUSTRIES
OF THE
LOS ANGELES AREA

© Copyright 1960 by Map Projects Inc.

Aircraft
Automobiles
Brewing
Building materials
Canning
Cement
Chemicals
Clothing
Electrical equipment
Flour milling
Food processing
Furniture
Household appliances
Lumber milling

La Mesa

Lemon
Grove

San Diego

Coronado
National City

Chula
Vista

INDUSTRIES
OF THE
SAN DIEGO AREA

© Copyright 1960 by Map Projects Inc.

MAJOR
MINERALS

San Francisco

LOS ANGELES

San Diego

Borax   Natural gas

Cement   Oil
materials

Copper   Silver

Gold   Tungsten

Iron

0   100
Miles

Machinery
Meat packing
Motion pictures
Oil
Oil refining
Paper and pulp
Printing and publishing
Resorts
Shipbuilding
Shipping
Sugar refining
Textiles
Tires
Wine

Water Supply

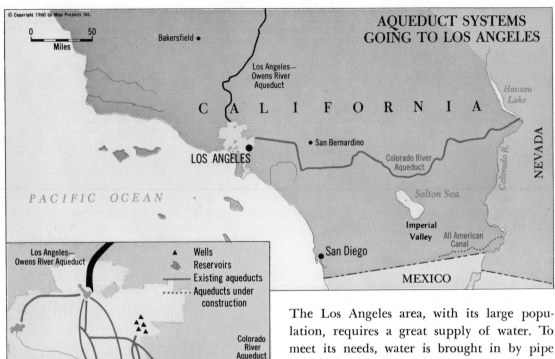

The Los Angeles area, with its large population, requires a great supply of water. To meet its needs, water is brought in by pipe lines from long distances.

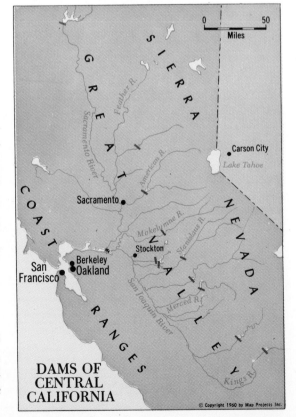

Little moisture falls on the Central Valley in the dry season. During the seasons of rainfall, water is dammed and stored. It is released through canals when needed to irrigate the fields where farming is carried on.

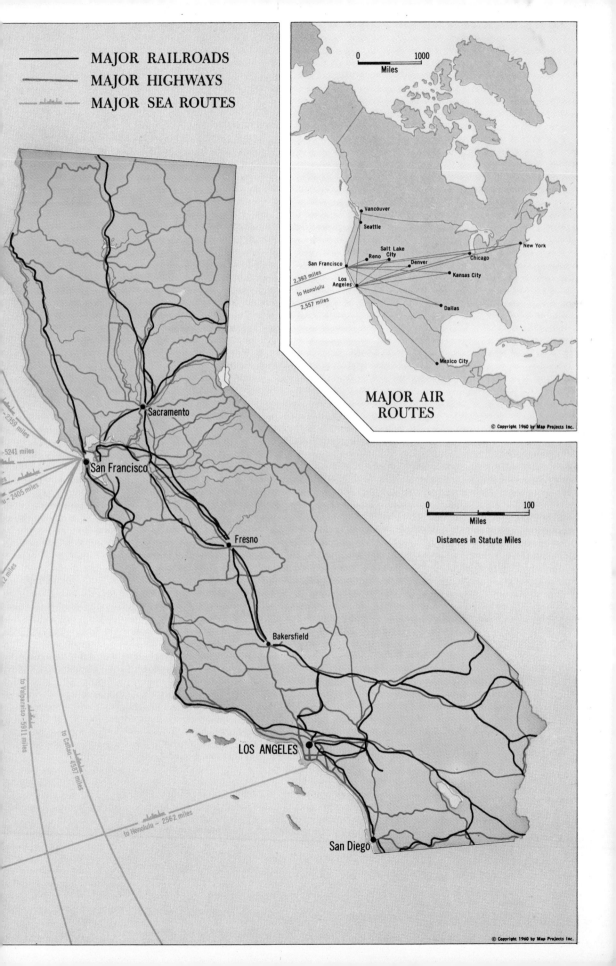

MAJOR RAILROADS

MAJOR HIGHWAYS

MAJOR SEA ROUTES

MAJOR AIR
ROUTES

© Copyright 1960 by Map Projects Inc.

Sacramento

San Francisco

Fresno

Bakersfield

LOS ANGELES

San Diego

0   1000
Miles

0   100
Miles

Distances in Statute Miles

Vancouver

Seattle

Salt Lake
City
Reno

San Francisco   Denver   Chicago   New York

Los
Angeles   Kansas City

Dallas

Mexico City

2,393 miles
to Honolulu

2,557 miles

to Valparaiso – 5911 miles

to Callao – 4587 miles

to Honolulu – 2562 miles

— 2359 miles

– 5241 miles

u – 2405 miles

lulu – 2 miles

© Copyright 1960 by Map Projects Inc.

Union Pacific Railroad

A land of great variety, California has about six different zones of climate. It has high mountains, broad valleys, arid deserts, and more than 1000 miles of seacoast. Shown above is Midway Point on the Monterey Peninsula. Below is a scene in the great Central Valley.

Western Growers Ass'n

The two largest deserts in California are the Mojave and the Colorado. Near Badwater in Death Valley is the lowest point in the United States, about 282 feet below sea level.

Only sixty miles away from Badwater is Mount Whitney, the highest point in continental United States. Rising 14,496 feet high, it is part of the 400-mile long Sierra Nevada Range.

INDEX

Asterisks refer to maps. Page numbers in italics refer to captions.